5

INGREDIENT FIX

5

INGREDIENT
FIX

EASY, ELEGANT, *and*
IRRESISTIBLE RECIPES

CLAIRE
ROBINSON

GRAND CENTRAL
Life & Style
NEW YORK • BOSTON

Grand Central Life & Style
Hachette Book Group
237 Park Avenue
New York, NY 10017

www.HachetteBookGroup.com

Grand Central Life & Style is an imprint of Grand Central Publishing.
The Grand Central Life & Style name and logo are trademarks of Hachette Book Group, Inc.

Printed in the United States of America

First Edition: October 2010
10 9 8 7 6 5 4 3 2 1

Library of Congress Cataloging-in-Publication Data

Robinson, Claire.
  5 ingredient fix: easy, elegant, and irresistible recipes / Claire Robinson.
    p. cm.
  Includes index.
  ISBN 978-0-446-57209-5
  1. Quick and easy cookery. 2. Entertaining. I. Title. II. Title: Five ingredient fix.
  TX833.5.R623 2010
  641.5'55—dc22

                          2010016495

Design by Gary Tooth / Empire Design Studio

On this food adventure

of mine, I've had a guide who has steered me every step of the way.
Elijah, you lived your life by your own set of rules, never letting a moment
pass you by without acknowledging it. Forever chasing life, you
were authentic in everything you did, every friendship you held, and every
belief you practiced. You showed me the essence of a truly lived life can
be found in something as exhilarating as jumping out of a plane, and in
something as simple as cooking dinner.

Without your incredible spirit, food wouldn't taste half as good and this
journey wouldn't be nearly as sweet. You inspired me to leap from great
heights and cook up my own life. This book is for you.

A Letter to My Readers

AS A GIRL, I USED TO SIT GLUED TO THE TELEVISION watching my early teachers Julia, James, and Jacques create magic on-screen. I always chose cooking shows over cartoons, much preferring the magical sounds of the kitchen to *Scooby Doo*.

Perhaps this is why I paid such close attention to the cooking and entertaining that went on in my own home. I can still see my grandmother running around the house before a party, making last-minute touches just before the guests arrived: the magnolia and forsythia peppering the dining and living room just so; the table settings as elaborate as anything I'd ever seen (my favorites: the gigantic ceramic horse heads that came out of hibernation for her annual Kentucky Derby party, or the enormous collection of coral and sea glass that covered the table when seafood was on the menu); what seemed like a hundred mirrors and oil-filled glass tapered candlesticks of different heights running down the length of the table. It was enchanting.

My Mama Neida was such an incredible, beautiful woman in every way, and anyone who walked through that front door was made to feel like the most important person in the world (and, of course, she made the entire night seem effortless). My grandfather was the president of the University of Memphis, so there were lots of parties, and it was *always* entertaining at its best. Back then, throwing a dinner party meant a lot of work, but Mama Neida loved to "fudge" the details. She was not a cook—a businesswoman and a social butterfly, yes, but definitely not a cook. Most of her events were carefully themed and catered or stocked with prepared food purchases. But she did have a small arsenal of recipes that rotated through her many dinner party menus, like Smothered Quail with Rice and English Peas (so simple but one of my

favorites), Bacon-Wrapped Oysters Baked on Rock Salt, and, to cap it off, the best little individual Pecan Tarts. Her advice to me was always, learn how to make a handful of dishes well. She pulled off the delicate balance between presentation, ease, and home cooking with grace, and no one ever suspected she'd "fudged" a thing.

My mother, on the other hand, has a traveler's heart and entertaining was never her forte. With her hippie spirit she didn't allow candy or junk food in the house, somehow convincing two children to believe carob-coated protein bars were candy. (They're not bad, I swear!) She even made her own baby food for my brother and me, pureeing boiled, fresh, seasonal ingredients. Mom would let me sit on the countertop and I would "assist" while she made pita bread, éclairs, or even egg rolls—all from scratch. We had dinner at the table as a family every night, even when I was in high school and wanted to be out with friends.

My mother has lived everywhere, even for a short while in a cave in Greece (did I mention she was a hippie?), and her rotating repertoire of recipes reflects her globe-trotting days. When we were growing up, dinner might have been roasted chicken with mashed potatoes one night, lamb shish kebobs with tahini sauce and couscous the next night, followed by homemade pizzas—dough and all—the next. (My brother and I always like to top a pizza with extra "foo foo dust," which was just ground fennel seed—I'm pretty sure you won't find that at your local pizza parlor.) Mother would spend hours in the kitchen making all kinds of different breads or an out-of-this-world cheesecake with laundry lists of ingredients and steps. I'm sure the grocery shopping alone took half the day.

And then there's my style—the result of learning from a classic entertainer and a do-it-from-scratch, all-natural bohemian. I take the best parts of these women, throw in my French culinary education, pay attention to seasonal ingredients, keep it fresh, and add my wholesome and delicious southern taste. This is my world of food: one inspired by an effortless elegance, and my five-ingredient approach keeps it simple (and possible!) for everyone. My life has been a never-ending exploration of the world of food as culture and entertainment, and I am the luckiest person in the world to be able to share this adventure with you.

Xo,
Claire

5

INGREDIENT FIX

5 Ingredient Philosophy

WOULD YOU BELIEVE ME IF I SAID SCALLOPS changed my life? When I was a student at the French Culinary Institute one of my teachers presented our class with a beautiful display of fresh scallops and gave us a challenge: come up with the best way to cook them. Simple enough, right? I remember all of us digging through the pantry, grabbing spices, vegetables, herbs, sweating to come up with innovative and daring combinations that would wow our professor, someone who'd truly seen it all in his many years of teaching.

We each presented him with our creations, and after he'd dutifully tasted each one, he let us in on a little secret— or rather, a big secret. Turns out his simple challenge was met with a very simple answer: the best way to cook fresh, in-season scallops is to throw them in a dry pan with some salt and pepper. No oil, no fancy herbs, no elaborate sauce… nothing. As the scallops sear, they release their own beautiful flavors—that sweet, rich taste that you either love or you don't, but that really is the core of the scallop. It was a straight-forward lesson, but a total game changer for me. From that day on I understood that the more ingredients you use, the greater risk you run of losing the essential flavor of your food.

This was my first and most important lesson in simpli-fication, one that I've made the cornerstone of my cooking philosophy. When your ingredients are good, there's no need to mask and muddle the flavor with unnecessary add-ons. I always want to know what my food really tastes like. My focus ever since that day was learning how to choose the best main ingredient—my star—and figuring out how to enhance and maintain its natural flavor by adding a small supporting cast of ingredients to dance with it and make it shine. After years of cooking, playing, experimenting, and learning, I've found that my magic number of ingredients is five or fewer.

What this means is that you have to cook food at its best, which means buying food at its best. Sure, you could make my Grandma Moore's Creamed Corn (page 164) with frozen corn (I've done it!), but you'd have to add a ton of cream and sugar just to mimic those natural flavors and juices found in fresh, height-of-season summer corn. Not sure what produce is in-season? Here's a little hint: when you walk into your grocery store, notice what's immediately on display in the produce section. Peaches piled sky-high right as you enter the store? Their price slashed? The abundance lets you know that they're in season and they're ready for you. Sometimes it's about grocery shopping with an open mind and choosing your ingredients before you settle on a recipe. My advice next time you see that pile of peaches is to buy a whole bunch and make my Smoky Roasted Peaches (see page 161)!

Let the seasons help you decide what to cook, and be sure to talk to the people you're buying from—they're the experts, and they'll know what's good, what's fresh, and what's ripe for the picking. The better the main ingredient, the less you're going to have to add to it to make a delicious dish. The bottom line is, I don't want you to work so hard! Simplify your cooking and you'll be amazed at what one ingredient can really do.

And here's another amazing trick: the way you cook something can totally transform its flavor. I go to the farmer's market, buy handfuls of beautiful, green haricots verts, and come up with fifty ways to cook them just by changing a few of the secondary ingredients. The dish is different every time, but the haricots verts always remain the star.

Technique is equally important. Take garlic, for example. You like it bitter? Fry it. You want that pungent, intense flavor? Sauté it. Prefer it sweet and melt-in-your-mouth good? Roast it. All the methods make the garlic taste totally different, and it's just a testament to the varying flavors you have the power to unlock in your food.

Each ingredient should truly stand out in a recipe, and with five or fewer ingredients, you're really going to taste the food you're cooking. My dishes are ones that are simple to shop for, easy to prepare, and fun to serve, and they promote healthy, seasonal eating. By following my recipes you'll wind up with lighter grocery bags, a heavier wallet, an uncluttered kitchen, and, most important, delicious meals to share with your family and friends.

Happy Cooking!

The Basics Every Kitchen Warrior Should Own

CONTRARY TO WHAT YOU HEAR FROM ALL THE TELEVISION shows, infomercials, advertisements, and catalogs, a savvy cook needs only a few basic tools and supplies to be a real master of the most popular room in the house. Five-ingredient cooking will streamline your time in the kitchen, and there's no need to clutter the cabinets with excess gadgets and unused products. My cooking style not only uses simple ingredients, but minimal tools. Here is a basic list of the tools, equipment, and supplies I couldn't live without!

COOKING EQUIPMENT

- 4 skillets: 2 large skillets—one 10- or 12-inch and one large nonstick; and 2 small skillets—one 6- or 8-inch and one small nonstick (omelet pan)
- Cast-iron skillets (optional): these are great if you have them; they can also serve as nonstick if they are well-seasoned
- 2 saucepans: one large (3- or 4-quart) and one small (1 quart), with lids
- 1 large (8- to 12-quart) stock/soup pot with lid
- One 8- to 10-quart Dutch oven
- 2 large (11 × 17-inch) sheet pans
- 1 large roasting pan with a rack
- 1 grill pan
- 1 large colander
- 1 cooling rack
- 1 muffin tin

- Two 8- or 9-inch cake pans
- 2 casserole/baking dishes
- 1 mixing bowl set

KNIVES

- One 8- or 10-inch chef's knife
- One 6-inch paring knife
- 1 large serrated knife
- 1 boning knife
- 1 sharpening steel or whetstone

SMALL WARES

- One 2-cup-capacity glass liquid measuring cup
- 1 set of dry measuring cups
- 1 set of measuring spoons
- Wooden spoons
- Rubber spatulas
- Whisk
- Fish spatula

- Metal tongs
- 2 fine-mesh strainers (1 small, 1 large)
- Microplane zester
- Box grater
- Vegetable peeler
- Can opener
- Rolling pin
- Kitchen shears
- Pastry brush
- Pepper grinder
- Plastic cutting boards for meat
- Large wooden cutting board

SMALL APPLIANCES

- Blender
- Food processor

SUPPLIES

- Aluminum foil
- Plastic wrap
- Parchment paper
- Kitchen string
- Resealable plastic bags
- Plastic storage containers

BASIC FOOD PANTRY ITEMS

- Olive oil
- Balsamic vinegar, white and red
- Chicken stock
- Unbleached all-purpose flour
- Granulated sugar
- Honey
- Grade B maple syrup
- Dried fruits
- And, of course, salt and pepper

WHAT I LIKE TO CALL "DOUBLE-DUTY INGREDIENTS"

I keep a few ingredients on hand that offer double the flavor and have more than one use, to keep my five-ingredient cooking versatile and simple:

- Infused olive oils, such as garlic, lemon, and chili
- Self-rising flour
- Spice blends, such as BBQ or Creole/Cajun (Be sure to check sodium content when buying spice blends.)

1.

UP AND AT 'EM

BREAKFAST ON THE TABLE WITH 5

Breakfast has always been my favorite meal.
It's that perfect balance of savory and sweet that
fills you up and tastes like a treat at the same
time, and maybe that's why I like breakfast any
time of day. And if you're anything like me (not
a morning person), breakfast better be worth
waking up for! Who wouldn't want to get out
of bed for Maple Candied Bacon?

MAPLE CANDIED BACON

1 pound good-quality
thick-sliced bacon

½ cup pure Grade B maple syrup

1 teaspoon Dijon mustard

Finely ground black pepper,
to taste

YIELD: 4 TO 6 SERVINGS

What makes this recipe really sing:
Dijon mustard has a nice vinegary bite
that cuts through the saltiness of the
bacon. Grade B syrup, richer in flavor,
is the only syrup I use.

What to toss in if you have it:
Throw a pinch of chili powder or
smoked paprika into the syrup mix for
added zip. Make extra of this stuff—
it flies off the plate.

Preheat the oven to 400°F.

Line a rimmed baking sheet with heavy foil. Place a baking rack over the lined sheet pan and arrange the bacon slices across the rack next to each other, not overlapping.

In a small bowl, whisk the maple syrup and mustard. Generously spoon over the top of the bacon, and bake 12 to 15 minutes. Turn the bacon over and baste with the syrup mixture. Bake an additional 5 to 10 minutes, or until the bacon has reached desired crispiness.

Carefully remove the sheet pan from the oven. Sprinkle the hot bacon with a scant pinch of finely ground black pepper. Let the bacon rest on the rack for 5 minutes before serving.

PUMPKIN SEED DRIED-CHERRY TRAIL MIX

Preheat the oven to 300°F.

Line two baking sheets with parchment paper or silicone baking mats.

In a large bowl, toss the pumpkin seeds, almonds, and sunflower seeds with the syrup until evenly coated. Spread the nuts and seeds out in an even, single layer on the lined baking sheets and season with salt. Bake them, stirring several times with spatula or wooden spoon, until just golden, about 20 minutes. Cool the nuts and seeds completely on the sheet tray, then add the cherries and toss to combine.

Store the cooled trail mix in an airtight container at room temperature for up to two weeks.

2 cups baby pumpkin seeds (pepitas)

1 cup slivered almonds

3/4 cup raw sunflower seeds

6 tablespoons pure Grade B maple syrup

Coarse salt, to taste

1 cup dried cherries or cranberries

YIELD: ABOUT 6 CUPS

What makes this recipe really sing:
This is the perfect combination of crunchy, soft, salty, and sweet; it's fantastic on yogurt or as a quick energy snack before a workout.

What to toss in if you have it:
Any other nuts you have to throw in will make it even more addictive—even salted peanuts. For a real treat, toss in finely chopped chunks of bittersweet chocolate.

DECONSTRUCTED SWEET POTATO HASH with FRIED EGGS

Melt 4 tablespoons butter in a large skillet over medium-high heat. Add 4 sage leaves and fry quickly until crisp, about 30 seconds. Transfer to a paper towel–lined plate to drain.

Add the sweet potatoes to the skillet, toss until coated in butter, and then add the water and remaining 8 sage leaves. Bring the water to a simmer and cook the potatoes, uncovered, until water has evaporated and potatoes are just fork-tender, about 10 minutes. If there is any excess water in the pan, remove it with a large spoon and reserve. Continue cooking the potatoes, scraping the pan frequently with a spoon, until crusty brown, about 10 more minutes. Add a tablespoon of the leftover cooking liquid or fresh water if the potatoes stick or begin to scorch.

Meanwhile, melt 2 tablespoons butter in medium skillet over medium heat. Add the chopped onions and cook, adding water as necessary when the pan gets dry, until deep golden brown, about 20 minutes. Transfer the onions to a serving bowl. Wipe out the pan, add the remaining 2 tablespoons butter, and fry the eggs, 2 at a time, to your preference (I like mine over easy).

Plate the potatoes in the center of four plates with the caramelized onions beside them. Top each plate with 2 fried eggs, garnish with a fried sage leaf, and enjoy!

¼ pound (1 stick) unsalted butter, divided

12 fresh sage leaves, divided

2 medium sweet potatoes, peeled and cut into ½-inch cubes

1 cup water plus more as needed

2 Vidalia or sweet onions, chopped

8 large eggs

YIELD: 4 SERVINGS

What makes this recipe really sing:
Sage, probably my hands-down favorite herb, gets a boost from a quick fry in the hot butter. It adds a little crunch to the creamy egg yolks and soft, pillowy sweet potatoes.

What to toss in if you have it:
A spicy Italian breakfast sausage or lamb merguez will round out the plate and make the onions taste even sweeter.

SPINACH and EGGS en COCOTTE

1 1/2 pounds spinach leaves, woody stems removed

1 cup heavy cream

Kosher salt and freshly cracked black pepper, to taste

1/4 cup grated Pecorino Romano cheese plus more for garnish

Freshly grated nutmeg, to taste

8 large eggs

YIELD: 4 SERVINGS

What makes this recipe really sing:
Creamed spinach for breakfast? Need I say more? Pecorino Romano is a great alternative to Parmesan; it's sharper and is great on creamy pastas or eggs.

What to toss in if you have it:
Brown some maple breakfast sausage and toss it with the spinach before baking the eggs; and, of course, have a toasted English muffin on the side to soak up all the yummy egg yolk and creamy spinach.

Preheat the oven to 425°F.

Fill a large pot with 1 inch of water and place a vegetable steamer basket inside. Bring the water to a boil over medium-high heat; add the spinach, cover, and cook until spinach is wilted, 3 to 4 minutes. Using tongs, squeeze the excess water from the spinach leaves and transfer them to a skillet. Add the cream, season with salt and pepper, and simmer over medium heat until cream has nearly evaporated, 10 to 12 minutes. Stir in 1/4 cup Pecorino Romano and nutmeg to taste.

Transfer the spinach to four oven-safe single-serving chafing dishes or four wide 8-ounce ramekins set on a baking sheet.

Make an indentation in the center of the spinach in each dish and crack 2 eggs into the center of each dish. Cover each dish tightly with aluminum foil. Bake in the center of the oven until the whites are set completely, approximately 6 to 12 minutes.

Remove from the oven, season with salt and pepper, and sprinkle a little grated Pecorino Romano cheese over each. Serve immediately.

BRIOCHE FRENCH TOAST
with STRAWBERRIES and CREAM

3 cups fresh strawberries, trimmed and sliced

2 tablespoons water

6 large eggs

2 cups heavy cream, divided

1 pat unsalted butter

Eight 1-inch-thick slices brioche (from a day-old loaf)

YIELD: 4 TO 6 SERVINGS

What makes this recipe really sing:
Although you can make French toast with any bread—even hot dog buns—splurging for a buttery, eggy brioche or challah bread sends this breakfast classic over the top.

What to toss in if you have it:
A splash of pure vanilla extract in the custard and a pinch of cinnamon will make this dessert-worthy. Pick your favorite berries at their seasonal peak and toss them with the strawberry syrup and sprinkle toasted sliced almonds over the plate.

Preheat the oven to 200°F and warm an ovenproof serving platter in the oven.

In a medium saucepan, combine 2 cups berries with the water and bring to a simmer. Cook over medium heat until the berries are softened and set aside until ready to serve. Keep warm.

In a shallow bowl, large enough to soak a few slices of bread, whisk together the eggs and 1 cup cream.

In a large nonstick griddle or skillet over medium heat, melt a large pat of butter. Be sure to cover the cooking surface with the melted butter. Working in batches, dip however many slices of brioche that can be cooked on the griddle at a time in the egg-cream mixture. Turn the slices over and be sure not to let them get too soggy.

Transfer the bread to the preheated and buttered griddle and cook until golden brown and slightly crisp, about 3 minutes per side. Place the cooked French toast on the warm serving platter in the oven and cover loosely with foil. These will keep warm in the oven while the remaining slices are prepared.

Whip the remaining 1 cup cream, in a medium bowl, with a hand-held mixer, until soft peaks form.

Serve the French toast topped with the warm strawberries, remaining sliced fresh strawberries, and whipped cream.

BREAKFAST CROQUE MADAME

Put the cheese in the freezer for 20 minutes to make it easier to slice.

Preheat the oven to 350°F.

Halve the croissants horizontally and toast them in the oven 10 minutes, or in a toaster oven. Spread a light layer of butter on each half and set aside.

Melt 2 tablespoons butter over medium-low heat. Crack the eggs into a bowl, season with salt and pepper, and whisk well. Pour the eggs into a large skillet and cook gently, stirring constantly, until creamy and set but not dry.

Remove the cheese from the freezer and cut into thin slices with a sharp knife.

To build the croque madame, put 1 ounce of ham on the bottom half of each croissant. Top each with ¼ of the scrambled eggs, followed by ¼ of the cheese; place the croissant top halves in place, transfer the sandwiches to a baking sheet, and heat in the oven until the cheese is beginning to melt and the sandwiches are hot, 5 to 10 minutes. Serve warm.

4 ounces triple-cream cheese, such as St. Andre, Brie, or Explorateur

4 croissants

4 tablespoons unsalted butter, divided

8 large eggs

Kosher salt and freshly cracked black pepper, to taste

4 ounces thinly sliced rosemary-steamed or smoked ham, or your favorite ham

YIELD: 4 SERVINGS

What makes this recipe really sing:
A classic croque madame has ham, Gruyère, and a fried egg. I've sent this version to another level with buttery croissants and triple-cream cheese; once you've had eggs with Brie or Explorateur, you'll never use that pregrated, bagged cheddar again.

What to toss in if you have it:
A tablespoon of chopped chives in the eggs will truly make this breakfast sandwich fit for a queen!

BAKED FRESH RICOTTA
with STEWED CHERRIES

Preheat the oven to 350°F.

Put the ricotta in a fine-mesh strainer set over a bowl and let stand 10 minutes to remove excess liquid. Transfer the cheese to a bowl; add the egg, 1 tablespoon honey, the salt, and half the lemon zest and stir until well combined. Transfer to an 8-ounce shallow baking dish and place on a baking sheet. Bake in the center of the oven until puffed and beginning to brown, about 35 minutes. Remove from the oven and let stand 10 minutes before serving.

Meanwhile, put the cherries, lemon juice and remaining zest, and 2 tablespoons honey in a small saucepan. Bring to a simmer over medium heat and cook until thickened and the cherries are broken down, about 15 minutes.

Serve the ricotta spread over toast or English muffins and top with stewed cherries.

1 1/2 cups fresh whole milk ricotta cheese

1 large egg

3 tablespoons honey, divided

1/2 teaspoon kosher salt

Zest and juice of 1 lemon, divided

6 ounces fresh dark cherries, pitted and quartered

YIELD: 4 SERVINGS

What makes this recipe really sing:
This is a fantastic, warm alternative to yogurt and fruit. Baking the ricotta removes moisture, turning this into a sort of cheesecake-for-breakfast treat without all the fat.

What to toss in if you have it:
Stir some fresh blueberries and raspberries into the stewed cherries when you remove them from the heat for a fresh, sweet burst of juicy flavor. A scoop of the cheese and fruit is great on waffles or with a bagel.

SMOKED SALMON and PUMPERNICKEL STRATA

12 large eggs

4 ounces crème fraîche, divided

Kosher salt and freshly cracked black pepper, to taste

2 large slices (about 3 ounces) pumpernickel bread, lightly toasted and torn into 1-inch pieces

4 ounces sliced smoked salmon

2 tablespoons drained capers

YIELD: 4 TO 6 SERVINGS

What makes this recipe really sing:
Pumpernickel, smoked salmon, and capers is a classic combination in any bagel shop in New York, but it's the crème fraîche, with its creamy, velvety texture and tart flavor, that turns plain eggs into a breakfast fit for a four-star hotel.

What to toss in if you have it:
Although the capers add a tart bite, some finely minced red onion scattered over the strata will add a savory kick that is a great partner with the salty salmon.

Preheat the oven to 350°F.

Line the bottom of an 8-inch square cake pan with parchment paper.

Whisk the eggs and 2 ounces crème fraîche in a large bowl and season well with salt and pepper. Add the pumpernickel cubes and let stand 20 minutes, until the bread has soaked up some of the egg and softened. Pour the mixture into the lined pan and bake until the eggs are just set, 25 to 30 minutes.

Let the strata stand for 10 minutes to cool slightly. Run a knife around the edges and cut into 6 to 8 pieces and transfer to a serving platter.

Serve the strata with the remaining crème fraîche, smoked salmon, and capers on the side as garnish for your guests.

ROASTED PLUMS
with GREEK YOGURT

8 fresh black plums, halved
and pitted

1 tablespoon unsalted butter

3 tablespoons honey

½ teaspoon ground cinnamon

Pinch of kosher salt

Fat-free Greek yogurt

YIELD: 4 SERVINGS

What makes this recipe really sing:
Roasting fruit helps concentrate their
juices and natural sugars. It's particularly
helpful to roast fruit that are not
at their seasonal peak to coax more
flavors out of them.

What to toss in if you have it:
Sprinkle your favorite organic granola
or a few handfuls of toasted almonds
and walnuts for a complete breakfast
full of protein.

Preheat the oven to 400°F.

Put the plums cut side up in a baking dish. Melt the butter in a small
saucepan, whisking in the honey, cinnamon, and a pinch of salt. Drizzle
the hot honey butter over the plums and roast in oven until very soft,
about 12 minutes.

Spoon the warm plums and sauce over yogurt and serve immediately.

HOMEMADE MAPLE BREAKFAST SAUSAGE

Combine all the ingredients and wrap tightly with plastic wrap. Chill in the refrigerator for at least an hour and up to overnight.

When ready to cook, form the mixture into small patties about ¼-inch thick and 3-inches wide; cook in a skillet over medium-high heat, turning once, until golden brown and completely cooked through, about 8 minutes total. Serve warm.

1 ½ pounds ground pork shoulder

2 tablespoons Grade B maple syrup

1 teaspoon dried sage

1 shallot, finely chopped

1 tablespoon Dijon mustard

1 teaspoon freshly cracked black pepper

1 teaspoon kosher salt

YIELD: 4 TO 6 SERVINGS

What makes this recipe really sing:
The nice thing about making your own sausage is you control the fat and seasonings. If you want it spicy, go for it with a couple pinches of chili flakes. You don't need a meat grinder to make sausage, just buy the pork already ground or have your butcher grind it.

What to toss in if you have it:
This sweet and savory sausage is great with some very finely diced apple (added to it before cooking), which will make the sausage moister and sweeter. If you like Italian sausage, add a teaspoon of fennel seeds.

BROWN BUTTER BANANA MUFFINS

¼ pound (1 stick) unsalted butter

4 ripe bananas

⅓ cup raw agave syrup or honey

1 large egg

1 ¾ cups self-rising flour

YIELD: 12 MUFFINS

What makes this recipe really sing:

Agave syrup, made from the same plant tequila is made from, adds a warm sweetness to these moist muffins. Be sure to use very ripe bananas, as the riper they are the less starchy and sweeter they become.

What to toss in if you have it:

Chopped toasted pecans will add a nice crunch; a smear of cream cheese on a warm muffin is heaven. Bagels begone!

Preheat the oven to 375°F.

Line a 12-cup muffin tin with paper muffin liners.

Put the butter in a small saucepan or skillet and melt over medium heat. Continue cooking, stirring occasionally, until the milk solids have turned a nutty golden brown; remove from the heat and let cool.

Peel the bananas and mash in a large bowl with a fork until liquefied. Add the agave syrup and egg and stir well; pour in the butter and whisk until completely combined. Add the flour and, with a rubber spatula, fold it into the wet ingredients until just combined; do not over mix. With an ice cream scoop, evenly divide the batter among the muffin tin cups.

Bake in the center of the oven until golden brown and the tops spring back when pressed, about 25 minutes. Cool for 5 minutes in the muffin tin; transfer the muffins to a rack to cool completely. Serve warm or at room temperature.

Note: *To make self-rising flour, add 1 ½ teaspoons baking powder and ½ teaspoon salt to 1 cup all-purpose flour.*

SPICED APPLE OATMEAL

Put the apples, water, honey, and salt in a large saucepan and bring to a boil over medium-high heat. Stir in the cereal, reduce the heat to a simmer, and cook according to the package instructions.

Meanwhile, put the butter in a small skillet and melt over medium heat. Continue cooking until the butter turns golden, nutty brown. Remove from the heat and stir in the pumpkin pie spice. Pour ¾ of the butter into the cereal and stir to combine; cover and let stand 10 minutes before serving.

To serve, divide the cereal among four bowls and drizzle some spiced brown butter over each serving.

1 cup packed dried apples (about 3 ounces), very finely diced

3 ¾ cups water

¼ cup honey

½ teaspoon salt

2 cups 5-grain cereal (or oatmeal)

6 tablespoons unsalted butter

¾ teaspoon pumpkin pie spice

YIELD: 4 SERVINGS

What makes this recipe really sing:
Cooking the butter until the milk solids turn golden draws out a rich nutty flavor that adds depth and richness to the cereal. You'll never find cereal this delicious in a diner!

What to toss in if you have it:
Dried fruit are a must-have in your pantry. Add some dried cherries and currants, and you'll have a hot cereal special enough for a holiday breakfast.

2.

It's Five O'Clock
SOMEWHERE

COCKTAILS AND NIBBLES FOR PARTIES OR ANYTIME

Well, I couldn't leave out cocktail hour, could I?
I'm a southern girl and five o'clock means getting
out on your porch with a beverage and your
family or friends to unwind and watch the world
go by. I keep my southern tradition going by
hosting many early-evening get-togethers just
for a drink and nibbles. Impress your guests with
Spicy Pecan and Parmesan Cheese Straws before
dinner, or a Cucumber-Watermelon Margarita
on a hot summer afternoon. I always have a few
nibbles, like Edamame Hummus or my Spicy
Citrus Mozzarella Bites, stored in the fridge for
impromptu moments. By all means, indulge
yourself at the end of a long day. Cheers!

POMEGRANATE-LEMON VODKA SPRITZERS

1 ½ cups pomegranate juice

1 cup freshly squeezed lemon juice plus 4 lemon wheels for garnish

½ cup granulated sugar

6 ounces citrus vodka

Seltzer water, for mixing

YIELD: 4 COCKTAILS

What makes this recipe really sing:
As with any recipe, cocktails benefit from the best ingredients. Ever had a margarita with that sweet and sour stuff in the plastic bottle? It's no substitute for real lime juice and sugar. Buy lemons when they are in season and inexpensive; squeeze the juice and freeze it; the taste of fresh lemon in cocktails makes a tremendous difference.

What to toss in if you have it:
This cocktail can easily be transformed into a martini; simply pour a splash of pomegranate juice, the lemon syrup, and vodka into an ice-filled cocktail shaker; shake until ice cold, and pour into a chilled martini glass rimmed with sugar. Cosmopolitan, step aside!

Pour the pomegranate juice into an ice cube tray and freeze overnight. Put the lemon juice and sugar in a small saucepan and bring to a simmer; cook, stirring, until sugar is completely dissolved. Cool to room temperature.

To serve, fill each of four tall rocks glasses with 3 to 4 pomegranate ice cubes; pour about ¼ cup lemon syrup and 1½ ounces vodka over the ice and top off with seltzer. Stir gently, garnish the glasses with lemon wheels, and serve.

Note: *This recipe is easily doubled or tripled for a crowd.*

APPLE SPICED BOURBON TODDYS

Put the cider, cinnamon, and star anise into a small saucepan and bring to a simmer over medium heat. Cook until the liquid has reduced by half and intensified in flavor, about 10 minutes. Add the lemon juice and bourbon and stir until hot.

Serve in warmed mugs or snifters each garnished with a cinnamon stick, star anise, and a maraschino cherry, if you have some!

1 quart fresh apple cider

1 cinnamon stick plus more for serving

2 whole star anise plus more for serving

Juice of 1 lemon

1 cup good-quality bourbon whiskey

Maraschino cherries, for garnish (optional)

YIELD: 3 COCKTAILS

What makes this recipe really sing:
Don't skimp on the fresh cider here. When the cider is simmered and thickened, the flavor is intensely apple, and intensely autumn! Star anise and cinnamon stick will fill your house with a delicious aroma—you might want to quadruple this recipe and keep it warm on the stove throughout a cold winter evening with friends.

What to toss in if you have it:
Throw a few slices of crisp apple and a squeeze of orange juice in the warm cider to brighten up the flavor. For a true toddy, float a pat of butter on each drink and relax by the fire.

GINGER MOJITOS

15 to 20 mint leaves plus
2 springs for garnish

2 tablespoons raw sugar plus
more for rimming the glasses

Juice of 1 lime plus 1 lime wedge

½ cup light rum

One 12-ounce bottle ginger beer

YIELD: 2 COCKTAILS

What makes this recipe really sing:
Ginger beer is strong in fresh ginger
flavor with a slightly spicy kick
and one of my favorite ingredients
to have on hand; it gives the drink
a little heat! If you cannot find ginger
beer, then use a natural ginger ale.
The refreshing flavor of the mint
and fresh lime juice with the hint
of ginger spice makes this the
perfect sipper!

What to toss in if you have it:
Place a large piece of candied ginger
directly in the drink before serving
or skewer a candied ginger piece on
a toothpick and lay it across the top
of the glass's rim. If you are a vodka
lover, try substituting the rum with a
ginger- or lime-flavored vodka.

Muddle the mint with 2 tablespoons raw sugar in a cocktail shaker.
Once the mint is broken down, add the lime juice and rum and fill the
shaker with ice. Run the lime wedge around the rims of two collins or
highball glasses and dip the rims into the raw sugar spread on a plate.
Shake the cocktail until ice cold and then carefully divide it between
the glasses, minding the sugared rims. Add more ice if necessary,
then top each glass off with ginger beer. Garnish each with a mint
sprig and enjoy!

KISS of JALAPEÑO BERRY BRAMBLE

Put the berries in a small bowl and sprinkle the sugar and lemon juice over them. Tuck the jalapeño into the mixture and let stand for 20 minutes; remove the jalapeño and gently mash the berries.

Overfill a lowball glass with crushed ice. Pour in the gin and then top with the berry mash, allowing dark color to streak the drink as it creeps into the crushed ice and gin. Serve with a straw.

½ cup blackberries

2 tablespoons granulated sugar

Juice of 1 lemon

1 jalapeño, cut in half and seeded

1 ½ ounces gin

YIELD: 1 COCKTAIL

What makes this recipe really sing:
This drink has it all—sweet blackberries, spicy jalapeño, smooth herbal gin. It's based on a classic English drink made with blackberries and gin, and once you try it, you'll be hooked.

What to toss in if you have it:
Sweet huckleberries are also awesome in this drink. In fact, a mixture of ripe dark berries would be terrific, along with using a splash of berry liqueur if you really like a sweeter drink.

ESPRESSO MARTINIS

3 ounces vanilla vodka

1 ounce dark crème de cacao

½ ounce Kahlúa

2 ounces brewed espresso

Softly whipped heavy cream,
for garnish

YIELD: 2 COCKTAILS

What makes this recipe really sing:
We are definitely in the age of the
designer cocktail, and this one will
truly impress your friends. The
combination of vanilla, chocolate,
and coffee flavors will satisfy those
latte-chugging friends during
cocktail hour.

What to toss in if you have it:
Shave some bittersweet chocolate
over the whipped cream and
add a sprinkling of cocoa for a
chocolate-caffeine blast. No mocha
tastes this good!

Put the liquors and espresso in a cocktail shaker filled with ice. Shake well until chilled; strain into two chilled martini glasses and float a layer of whipped cream over the tops.

CLAIRE'S NUTTY SIDECARS

Preheat the oven to 375°F.

Toast the hazelnuts on a sheet pan until you just begin to smell them, 5 to 7 minutes. Let them cool.

Put the hazelnuts and ¼ cup sugar into a mini food processor and pulse until finely ground. Pour the sugar-nut mixture onto a rimmed plate.

In a cocktail shaker, muddle the lemon chunks and remaining sugar until the chunks are broken down and very juicy and the sugar has dissolved. Add the cognac and Frangelico and fill the shaker with ice. Shake the mixture furiously to chip the ice and chill.

Run a lemon wedge around the rims of two 8-ounce rocks glasses and dip them in the sugar-nut mixture. Pour the liquors into the glasses, top off with more ice, garnish with lemon wedges, and serve immediately.

¼ cup shelled and skinned hazelnuts

¼ cup plus 1 heaping tablespoon granulated sugar

¾ lemon, cut into chunks and seeded, plus 3 lemon wedges for garnish

4 ounces cognac, such as Hennessy or Armagnac

2 ounces Frangelico

YIELD: 2 COCKTAILS

What makes this recipe really sing:
A good-quality cognac has a natural nutty flavor. The addition of Frangelico in the cocktail can also be delicious. Fresh lemon muddled with sugar adds a tart freshness.

What to toss in if you have it:
Use half the amount of lemon in each drink, replacing the rest with fresh orange pieces. For a lighter cocktail suitable as an aperitif, divide the mixed cocktail among four glasses and top each with seltzer water and stir.

A MOSCOW MULE in MIAMI

¼ cup fresh mint leaves plus a small bunch for garnish

2 teaspoons raw sugar

3 ounces vodka

Juice of 1 lime

3 ounces ginger beer

YIELD: 1 COCKTAIL

What makes this recipe really sing:
A variation on a mojito, this refreshing cocktail replaces the rum with vodka and the soda with spicy ginger beer. Super refreshing on a warm summer day!

What to toss in if you have it:
Toss a thin slice of peeled ginger into the cocktail shaker and muddle it with the mint and sugar for an extra-gingery kick.

In the bottom of a cocktail shaker, place ¼ cup mint and raw sugar and muddle. Top with vodka and lime juice; fill with ice and shake well. Pour the chilled, shaken drink through a bar strainer into a highball glass filled with ice and top with the ginger beer. Place a small bunch of mint on top for garnish.

CUCUMBER-WATERMELON MARGARITA

Liquefy the watermelon and cucumber in a blender and strain through a fine-mesh sieve and chill until ready to use.

Mix the lime zest and salt, pour onto a small plate, and reserve.

When ready to serve, mix ¼ cup watermelon-cucumber juice with the lime juice, agave, and tequila in a cocktail shaker filled with ice; shake well to chill. Rim a martini glass with the lime wedge and dip into the lime-zest salt. Pour the shaken margarita into the salt-rimmed martini glass and enjoy!

Note: *Leftover watermelon-cucumber juice can be stored in an airtight container in the refrigerator for up to 3 days.*

4 cups seedless
watermelon chunks

½ English cucumber, peeled
and coarsely chopped

Zest of 1 lime, juice of ½ lime
plus 1 lime wedge

¼ cup kosher salt

1 ounce agave syrup

3 ounces tequila

YIELD: 1 COCKTAIL

What makes this recipe really sing:
Watermelon juice and cucumber juice
are extremely good for you and
super refreshing on a hot summer day.
These delicious juices replace
the cloying sweet and sour mix found
in most restaurant margaritas
and the result is an addictive,
thirst-quenching cocktail.

What to toss in if you have it:
A splash of fresh orange juice or
a little Cointreau adds another fruity
element. If you have a whole
watermelon and cucumber, cut small
wedges of each for garnish.

ZUCCHINI-TINIS

ZUCCHINI WATER:

1 large zucchini

Kosher salt

ZUCCHINI-TINIS:

2 tablespoons simple syrup, (recipe follows)

2 tablespoons zucchini water

½ cup unfiltered sake, cold

¼ cup gin

2 thin, round slices zucchini per drink, for garnish

SIMPLE SYRUP:

1 cup granulated sugar

1 cup water

YIELD: 2 COCKTAILS

What makes this recipe really sing:
The floral, smooth flavor of unfiltered sake is a great match with gin. Add the mild, cucumberlike flavor of the zucchini, and you get an elegant, beautiful cocktail your guests will talk about for weeks.

What to toss in if you have it:
This cocktail is perfect for a fancy cocktail party or dinner; float a tiny organic orchid blossom in it for an extra-special event.

To make the zucchini water: Grate the zucchini on the large holes of a box grater and put it in a fine-mesh sieve over a bowl; sprinkle with a pinch of salt and let stand 15 minutes. Press the zucchini to extract as much water as possible.

To make the simple syrup: Put the sugar and water in a small saucepan and bring to a simmer over medium heat; stir until the sugar is completely dissolved. Cool and use immediately or store in an airtight container in the refrigerator up to 1 month.

To make the zucchini-tinis: Put the simple syrup, zucchini water, sake, and gin into a cocktail shaker filled with ice. Shake well and strain into two chilled martini glasses. Place the thinly sliced zucchini rounds on top as garnish. Serve and enjoy!

Note: *Leftover zucchini water can be stored in an airtight container in the refrigerator for up to 3 days.*

SPICY SPANISH DEVILED EGGS

Put the eggs in a saucepan and cover with cold water. Bring to a boil, then turn off the heat and cover. Let stand 10 minutes. Immediately run cold water over the eggs until completely cooled. Peel the eggs, halve them lengthwise, and transfer the yolks to a small bowl. Add the Dijon mustard, diced pepper, pickling liquid, paprika, and water and mash with a fork until smooth. Add more water until the yolk mixture is moist; season with salt and pepper and mix well.

Transfer the egg white halves to a serving platter. Lay a strip of Serrano ham into the indentation of each half, then fill the cavities with the yolk mixture. Sprinkle some paprika over the eggs to garnish and serve immediately.

12 large eggs

2 heaping tablespoons Dijon mustard

1 teaspoon finely diced pickled piquillo peppers plus 2 tablespoons liquid from the jar

1/4 teaspoon spicy Spanish smoked paprika plus more for garnish

2 tablespoons hot water, or as needed

Kosher salt and freshly ground black pepper, to taste

4 paper-thin slices Serrano ham, cut into 24 1/2-inch-wide strips

---

YIELD: 12 SERVINGS

What makes this recipe really sing:
The ever-popular deviled egg will never go out of style. Try my version; the spicy smoked paprika and piquillo peppers add the required spice and sweet vinegary bite, and the Serrano ham gives it a nice meaty, smoky finish. Look for canned piquillo peppers in brine in the olive-pickle section of the market or use Peppadew peppers.

What to toss in if you have it:
Finely mince a shallot and add it to the mashed yolks for a little onion flavor. For super rich deviled eggs, mash and add about 2 ounces of cream cheese to the filling until well combined before spooning into the egg whites.

EDAMAME HUMMUS

Bring a pot of salted water to a boil, add the edamame and garlic clove, and cook to package instructions; reserve ½ cup of the cooking liquid and strain. Put the edamame and garlic into a food processor along with lemon juice, tahini, coriander, and salt and pepper. Puree until smooth and, with the motor running, drizzle in ¼- to ½-cup cooking liquid to reach desired consistency. Taste for seasoning and adjust as necessary. Serve with crudités or toasted pita points.

2 cups frozen shelled edamame

1 garlic clove

Juice of 1 lemon

⅓ cup tahini

½ teaspoon ground coriander

Kosher salt and freshly cracked black pepper, to taste

¼ to ½ cup cooking water

Fresh vegetable crudités or toasted pita points, for serving

YIELD: 4 SERVINGS

What makes this recipe really sing:
Traditional hummus, made with chickpeas, is something I grew up eating and loving. I simply replaced the chickpeas with edamame and ended up with an addictive dip or spread that outshines its predecessor. A bit of ground coriander adds an exotic, almost Indian perfume to the dip.

What to toss in if you have it:
Sprinkle some finely diced seeded tomatoes over the top of the hummus along with a drizzle of basil or lemon olive oil. You really can take this base recipe and add spices and vegetables to your liking.

SPICY PECAN and PARMESAN CHEESE STRAWS

¼ cup pecan halves

¼ cup finely grated Parmesan cheese

2 teaspoons kosher salt

½ teaspoon smoked paprika

Freshly cracked black pepper, to taste

2 sheets frozen puff pastry, thawed, divided

YIELD: 6 SERVINGS

What makes this recipe really sing:
Store-bought puff pastry is the best shortcut I know. After sweating over puff pastry in culinary school, I realized I would never make it by hand again. These days there are several brands available, and with this easy recipe you can't fail to impress guests; cheesy, salty, crunchy . . . another drink, please?

What to toss in if you have it:
Puree some roasted, peeled red peppers with some cream cheese for a simple, quick dip for these spicy cheese straws.

Preheat the oven to 400°F.

Line a baking sheet with a silicone mat or parchment paper.

Put the pecans in the bowl of a mini food processor and pulse until fine (or hand chop). Add the Parmesan, salt, paprika, and pepper and pulse until well mixed.

Sprinkle ¼ of the nut mixture evenly onto a clean work surface and place 1 sheet of pastry directly on top. Sprinkle ¼ more of the nut mixture over the surface of the pastry. With a rolling pin, roll the pastry until the nut mixture has begun to stick into the dough. Fold the dough in half lengthwise and continue rolling until the nut mixture has been completely absorbed into the dough and the two sides of dough are stuck together.

With a pizza wheel, cut the folded edge from the dough and discard; cut ½-inch strips from the long side of the dough. Twist the strips five or six times and transfer them to the baking sheet. Repeat with the remaining sheet of pastry and nut mixture. Bake until puffed and golden brown, 15 to 20 minutes. Cool the straws completely on the baking sheet before serving.

FENNEL ORANGE CRACKERS

1 cup unbleached
all-purpose flour

1/2 cup whole-wheat flour
plus more for dusting

1 teaspoon kosher salt plus
more for sprinkling

1/4 cup extra-virgin olive oil

Zest of 1 navel orange plus 1/4 cup
freshly squeezed orange juice

2 tablespoons water

1 teaspoon fennel seeds

YIELD: 4 SERVINGS

What makes this recipe really sing:
I just love the combination of fennel
and orange; I have it together in
salads all the time. This ridiculously simple
recipe for homemade crackers turns that
combination into something crunchy and
wonderful to serve with wine or
cocktails along with some
soft cheese and olives.

What to toss in if you have it:
You can use any type of small seeds—
poppy seeds, celery seeds, or sesame
seeds—to sprinkle on these easy
crackers. You can also sprinkle a light
dusting of finely grated pecorino on the
dough just before baking. Spread
some fresh ricotta on it with a little more
orange zest, and you'll be a star at
your cocktail party.

Line two cookie sheets with parchment paper.

In a bowl, stir the flours and salt together until combined; make a well in the center with your hand. In another small bowl, whisk the olive oil, zest, orange juice, and water together and pour into the flour well. Using a fork, pull the flour into the liquid, whisking constantly, until the flour has absorbed most of it. Using your hands, knead the dough in the bowl until it comes together. Transfer the dough to a lightly floured counter and knead just until it will hold together in a ball. Wrap it tightly in plastic wrap and let the dough rest for 30 minutes.

Preheat the oven to 325°F.

Cut the dough in half. With a rolling pin on a lightly floured surface (dusted with whole-wheat flour), roll one half of the dough as thin as possible, about 1/16-inch thick. Sprinkle half the fennel seeds evenly over the dough and roll the rolling pin over it a couple of times to adhere the seeds. The dough can be cut into small round crackers with a cookie cutter, or rectangles or squares with a sharp knife. Transfer the cut dough to a baking sheet; gather up the scraps, reroll, and keep cutting crackers until the dough is used up. Repeat with the remaining dough half.

Transfer the sheets to the oven and bake, switching them halfway through, until light golden brown and crisp, about 15 minutes. Remove from the oven and cool the crackers completely on the sheets.

Once they're cool, serve them with your favorite dip or soft cheese.

Note: *The crackers can be stored in an airtight container or plastic bag up to 1 week.*

SPICY CITRUS MOZZARELLA BITES

8 ounces fresh cherry-size mozzarella balls (bocconcini), drained

1 teaspoon red pepper flakes

Zest of 1 lemon

3 tablespoons extra-virgin olive oil

1 tablespoon finely chopped fresh basil

Sea salt and freshly cracked black pepper, to taste

YIELD: 4 TO 6 SERVINGS

What makes this recipe really sing:
Simple, yet a perfect balance of acidity, heat, and creaminess, this has fast become a party staple. I love to serve these antipasti style alongside Marcona almonds, your favorite olive, and a salumi of choice. A perfect start to a meal at home or compliment to cocktails before heading to dinner.

What to toss in if you have it:
This is one of those perfect five ingredient recipes. Leave as is and enjoy!

Mix all the ingredients together in a bowl and serve immediately or chill in refrigerator until ready to eat.

ROSEMARY-PARMESAN SHORTBREAD

Put the flour, sugar, rosemary, salt, and Parmesan into the bowl of a food processor and pulse until combined. Add the butter and pulse just until a soft dough forms; the dough should hold together when squeezed with your hands. If it doesn't, add the water and pulse until combined. Spread a large sheet of plastic wrap on a work surface and transfer the dough onto it. Using the plastic wrap as a guide, form the dough into a loose log along one edge of the long side of the sheet. Roll the dough log, twisting the plastic gathered at the ends in opposite directions until the log is tight and compact, about 2½ inches in diameter.

Chill in the refrigerator until firm, about 1 hour.

Preheat the oven to 375°F.

Line two baking sheets with parchment sheets or silicone baking mats.

Slice the dough log into ⅓-inch-thick slices and place on the lined sheets, about 1 inch apart. Bake until the edges are just beginning to brown, 12 to 14 minutes.

Cool the slices on the sheet for 5 minutes, then transfer them to wire racks to cool completely. Store the shortbread in an airtight container at room temperature until ready to serve.

2 cups unbleached all-purpose flour

1 cup powdered sugar

2 teaspoons finely chopped fresh rosemary

½ teaspoon salt

½ cup finely grated Parmesan cheese

½ pound (2 sticks), unsalted butter, at room temperature

1 teaspoon water, if needed

YIELD: ABOUT 2½ DOZEN

What makes this recipe really sing:
These shortbread are a cross between a cookie and a cracker and are fantastic with wine or cocktails. They are both sweet from the sugar and savory from the rosemary and Parmesan, and are the perfect nibble for a predinner champagne toast.

What to toss in if you have it:
Spoon a little fresh ricotta on top of these and sprinkle some gray or pink sea salt over the top. Your guests will be surprised at the flavor and texture combination and will devour them.

3.

OPENING ACT

APPETIZERS TO START YOUR ENGINE

For me, appetizers always have a starring role.
Whether you're tiding guests over until dinner
or serving up tapas-style fare, apps are definitely
the most fun way to entertain. You never know
when you're going to have unexpected company
and with these easy recipes you can welcome the
spontaneity.

ASIAN BEEF ROLL-UPS

Juice of 2 limes

2 heaping tablespoons light brown sugar

3 tablespoons soy sauce

1 to 2 tablespoons chili sauce, or to taste (I recommend sriracha.)

1 pound flank steak

YIELD: 6 TO 8 SERVINGS

What makes this recipe really sing:
Flank steak has great beefy flavor but is a muscular cut of meat. It benefits from this acidic marinade, particularly when you cut the meat into strips before soaking it in the sweet, spicy, lime mixture, as this helps the acids permeate the meat and tenderize it quickly.

What to toss in if you have it:
Grill some whole scallions along with the meat strips, then chop them into 1-inch pieces. Roll a piece of scallion in the center of each beef strip for a smoky onion bite.

Whisk the lime juice, sugar, soy sauce, and chili sauce until combined in a glass baking dish. Slice the steak against the grain into very thin strips and place in the marinade, tossing to coat. Cover with plastic wrap and let stand at room temperature for 15 minutes.

Heat a nonstick grill pan over high heat until very hot. Working in batches, using tongs, drain the excess marinade from the meat strips into a bowl, quickly grill the steak, turning once, until seared and cooked through, 1 to 2 minutes total.

Meanwhile, pour the marinade into a small saucepan and bring to a simmer over medium heat. Cook until reduced and thickened, about 5 minutes.

Transfer the cooked beef to a cutting board. Roll each strip lengthwise into a bundle and spear each roll with a toothpick. Place the beef roll-ups on a platter and drizzle the thickened glaze over them. Serve immediately.

RIOJA-STEAMED MUSSELS
with CHORIZO

Put the chorizo in a large heavy pot with a lid over medium-high heat. Cook until the fat is rendered and the meat is browned, about 10 minutes. Remove the meat with a slotted spoon and reserve. Add the onion to the pot and cook until softened, 6 to 8 minutes. Add the chorizo back to the pot, pour in the wine, and bring to a boil. Drop in the mussels, cover, and cook until mussels have opened, 4 to 5 minutes.

Remove the lid and discard any mussels that have not opened. Season with pepper, add the parsley, and stir very well, until mixed, and mussels are coated in wine and onion slices. Serve immediately.

1 pound fresh chorizo, crumbled

1 large yellow onion, sliced

1 bottle Rioja or other dry red wine

2 pounds black mussels, cleaned and debearded

Freshly cracked black pepper, to taste

1/2 cup coarsely chopped curly parsley

YIELD: 4 SERVINGS

What makes this recipe really sing:
This is a fun Spanish spin on the classic moules meunière, or mussels with garlic and white wine. The spicy oils from the chorizo and sweet shallots pair super well with the mineral qualities of mussels; add the dry, robust flavor of Rioja, a Spanish red wine, and you'll never miss the French version.

What to toss in if you have it:
Classic steamed mussels are usually finished with parsley or other chopped herbs. If you like it spicy, mince a red chili and toss it, or a pinch of dried chili flakes, in with the shallots. Of course, the best part is the juice— you can slurp it up with the shells, or serve some thin toasted baguette slices or country bread alongside the dish for mopping up the liquid.

MUSHROOM CARPACCIO

½ pound large white mushrooms, brushed clean and trimmed

4 ounces baby arugula

Juice of 1 lemon

Extra-virgin olive oil, to taste

Kosher salt and freshly ground black pepper, to taste

Wedge of Parmesan cheese, for shaving

YIELD: 4 SERVINGS

What makes this recipe really sing:

This classic Italian appetizer is healthy, easy, and impressive. The taste of mushrooms with the spicy arugula, tart lemon, and green olive oil go fantastically well together, making a toothsome bite. Add the nutty, salty Parmesan and it's a five-ingredient combo you'll love to serve your guests. Use your best olive oil here; the grassy, herbaceous flavor of Tuscan or Greek olive oil is great for this dish.

What to toss in if you have it:

Some paper-thin strips of speck, a smoked prosciutto, or coppa, cured pork shoulder, will add some meaty saltiness. Very finely chopped boiled egg will match perfectly with the texture of the raw mushroom.

Using a mandoline or very sharp knife, slice the mushrooms as thinly as possible and arrange them in a single layer on a large serving platter. Scatter the arugula evenly over the top.

Just before serving, squeeze the juice of the lemon over the dish; very lightly drizzle some olive oil evenly over the mushrooms and greens. Season with salt and pepper and, using a vegetable peeler, shave thin strips of Parmesan evenly over the top. Serve immediately.

MINI SHRIMP CAKE POPPERS

In a large nonstick skillet, cook the bacon over medium heat until crisp and the fat has rendered, about 10 minutes. Transfer the bacon to a paper towel–lined plate to drain; remove the skillet from the heat to cool.

Put the shrimp into the bowl of a food processor and pulse until the shrimp are broken down but not mushy, about 20 seconds. Crumble the crisp bacon into the processor bowl, add the jalapeño, season with black pepper, and pulse again until the bacon is broken down and evenly distributed and the shrimp begins to form a ball. Do not overprocess.

Pour the bacon drippings from the skillet into a small bowl. Wipe out the residue in the skillet with a paper towel and return the skillet to medium-high heat. Add about 1 tablespoon of the drippings to the skillet. Working in batches and using a 1-ounce ice cream scoop or 2 tablespoons, drop balls of the shrimp mixture into the hot skillet. Wet the back of a spoon and press the balls into mini shrimp cakes, about ¼-inch thick. Cook until light golden, about 2 minutes. Flip the shrimp cakes and continue cooking them until firm and cooked through, another 1 to 2 minutes. Transfer them to a paper towel–lined plate to drain. Continue cooking the shrimp mixture until it is used up.

Stir the yogurt and chives together in a small bowl.

To serve, transfer the warm shrimp cakes to a serving platter, top each with a dollop of chive cream, and garnish with a few more chives.

3 slices smoked bacon

1 pound shrimp, peeled, deveined, and tails removed

½ small jalapeño, stemmed and seeds removed

Freshly cracked black pepper

½ cup nonfat Greek yogurt

1 tablespoon finely chopped chives plus more for garnish

YIELD: 1 ½ DOZEN

What makes this recipe really sing:
As they say, everything tastes better with bacon! This is a great one-bite appetizer for game day, a fancy cocktail party, or a Saturday evening get-together. It's a deconstructed shrimp and jalapeño popper, but much easier to make. The creamy yogurt is a cooling counterpart to the spicy shrimp and bacon bite.

What to toss in if you have it:
Although these cakes hold together and brown nicely when pan-seared, they can be rolled in flour or even panko bread crumbs for an extra-crunchy coating.

POLENTA "FRIES" with ROASTED TOMATO SAUCE

Bring the water to a boil in a large pot and add the salt. While whisking constantly, slowly drizzle in the cornmeal and whisk until smooth. Reduce the heat to medium and stir with a wooden spoon until the polenta is very thick and beginning to bubble, about 5 minutes. Remove from the heat and stir in the Parmesan cheese. Pour the mixture into a 9 × 12-inch rimmed sheet pan and smooth the surface. Let stand until cool, then refrigerate at least 2 hours.

Meanwhile, preheat the oven to 400°F.

Put the tomatoes and garlic on a rimmed baking sheet, drizzle the olive oil over them, season with salt and pepper, and toss to coat. Roast them in the oven, stirring occasionally, until the tomatoes have shriveled and are beginning to brown, 30 to 40 minutes. Transfer the tomatoes and garlic to a food processor and puree. Season to taste with salt and pepper, if needed. Put the sauce into a small cup and reserve.

Cut the chilled polenta into thin fingers, about ½-inch wide by 3 inches long. Working in batches, heat 2 tablespoons olive oil in a large nonstick skillet and shallow fry the polenta fries, turning to cook all sides, until browned, crisp, and heated through, about 10 minutes total. Transfer the fries to a paper towel–lined plate to drain and sprinkle with more grated Parmesan. Continue frying batches of polenta fingers, keeping the cooked ones warm in a low oven.

Serve the polenta fries warm with the tomato sauce for dipping.

4 cups water

1 teaspoon kosher salt plus more as needed

1 ½ cups coarse-ground cornmeal

½ cup freshly grated Parmesan cheese plus more as needed

4 cups grape tomatoes

2 garlic cloves

3 tablespoons extra-virgin olive oil

Freshly cracked black pepper, to taste

YIELD: 4 TO 6 SERVINGS

What makes this recipe really sing:
Roasting any vegetable will bring out its natural sugars, and grape tomatoes pack a load of flavor even before they release moisture in the oven and turn into sweet little morsels that can make you pucker.

What to toss in if you have it:
Polenta is creamy, rich, and satisfying, particularly if you use a good organic stone-ground brand of cornmeal. You can add even more flavor by cooking it in chicken stock; just be mindful that many store-bought brands of stock contain a lot of sodium. Look for low-sodium brands and keep them on hand for cooking.

MEAT PIES

12 frozen filo pastry sheets, thawed

4 tablespoons unsalted butter, divided

1 pound fresh bulk lamb sausage

1 Spanish onion, chopped

1/2 teaspoon ground cinnamon, plus more for dusting

Kosher salt and freshly cracked black pepper, to taste

YIELD: 3 DOZEN

What makes this recipe really sing:
These tasty little triangles are based on b'steeya, a delicious sweet and savory Moroccan flaky pie filled with shredded meat, nuts, and cinnamon and dusted with powdered sugar. Look for fresh lamb sausage at your butcher or gourmet market and feel free to experiment with different flavors. These are great with beer, wine, or fizzy cocktails.

What to toss in if you have it:
Add some currants or diced dried apricots to the filling, and for the real Moroccan flavor, dust them with powdered sugar just before serving. It is an unusual, delicious flavor combination that your guests will remember long after the party ends.

Preheat the oven to 400°F.

Line a baking sheet with parchment paper.

Lay the filo sheets on a work surface, short side closest to you. Cover them with a sheet of plastic wrap and then lay a damp towel over the plastic to keep the pastry from drying out.

Melt 2 tablespoons butter in a skillet over medium heat, add the sausage and cook, breaking it up with a spoon, until the meat is no longer pink, about 5 minutes. Add the onion and cook, stirring frequently, until it is translucent and the sausage is browned and broken down, 6 to 8 minutes. Stir in the cinnamon and taste the filling; add salt and pepper, if needed. Remove from the heat and cool to room temperature.

Melt the remaining butter in a small saucepan. Using a sharp knife, cut the filo into 3 × 11-inch strips, and re-cover with the towel. Using a pastry brush, brush 1 strip of filo with melted butter. Place a small spoonful of filling 1 inch from the end of the pastry. Fold the end over the filling to form a triangle; continue to fold up the strip in triangles, like folding up a flag.

Continue with remaining strips, placing the filled triangles on the baking sheet and keeping them covered with a towel until all are ready to bake.

Brush the triangles lightly with butter, and then bake 20 to 25 minutes, or until golden and crisp.

Serve the meat pies hot, sprinkled with a little more cinnamon, if desired.

ATTICUS' ASPARAGUS PESTO BITES

Bring the water to a boil and add the salt. While whisking constantly, slowly drizzle in the cornmeal and whisk until smooth. Reduce the heat to medium and stir with a wooden spoon until the polenta is very thick and beginning to bubble, about 5 minutes. Remove from the heat and stir in ½ cup Parmesan cheese. Pour the mixture into a 9 × 12-inch rimmed sheet pan and spread it out to a thickness of ½ inch. Let stand at room temperature until firm.

Bring a large pot of salted water to a boil; add the asparagus and cook until crisp-tender, about 4 minutes. Drain the asparagus and drop into a bowl of ice water to stop the cooking process. Once they're cool, trim the tips from the asparagus, slice them in half lengthwise and reserve; coarsely chop the stalks and transfer them to the bowl of a food processor. Add the remaining 1 cup Parmesan, pine nuts, and garlic oil and pulse the mixture until finely chopped; season with salt and pepper.

To serve, use a 2-inch round cookie cutter to punch out rounds of the firm polenta and transfer them to a platter. Top each polenta round with a spoonful of the asparagus mixture. Garnish with an asparagus tip and a few toasted pine nuts.

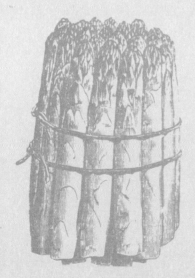

4 cups water

1 teaspoon kosher salt plus more as needed

1 ½ cups coarse-ground cornmeal

1 ½ cups freshly grated Parmesan cheese, divided

1 bunch asparagus (about 1 pound), trimmed

½ cup pine nuts, toasted, plus more for garnish

¼ cup garlic-flavored olive oil

Freshly cracked black pepper, to taste

YIELD: 4 TO 6 SERVINGS

What makes this recipe really sing:
Firm polenta makes a great base for appetizers; you can cut it into any shape and top it with just about anything, from olive tapenade to diced tomatoes with basil. Santino, a production manager on Food Network Challenge, whips up a version of these every party he and his wife host. I love the fun twist of asparagus pesto—the asparagus is just delicious with the creamy, rich polenta. My version is named after their baby boy with a huge appetite!

What to toss in if you have it:
Squeeze a little lemon juice into the food processor while pulsing the asparagus and add a little freshly grated zest to the top of each polenta bite with the pine nuts. If you have time, lightly sear the rounds in some olive oil until golden brown and crunchy for a great texture under the pesto.

FIG and ROSEMARY FLATBREAD

8 ounces frozen pizza dough, thawed

2 to 4 tablespoons garlic-flavored olive oil

2/3 cup fresh ricotta cheese

1/2 teaspoon finely chopped rosemary plus more for garnish

Kosher salt and freshly cracked black pepper, to taste

8 fresh or dried figs, quartered lengthwise through the stem

YIELD: 6 TO 8 SERVINGS

What makes this recipe really sing:
Ricotta, rosemary, and fig are a match made in heaven. Fresh, creamy ricotta is a somewhat neutral flavor, so a little splash of garlic oil brings it to life and pairs it beautifully with sweet figs and earthy rosemary.

What to toss in if you have it:
This combination of fig and rosemary works well not only on flatbread, but also can be used to top crostini, or wrapped in thin slices of prosciutto. Look for speck, a smoked prosciutto, in Italian delis and toss thin strips of it over the flatbread right after it comes out of the oven. A very thin drizzle of honey over the flatbread will enhance the ricotta and figs' sweetness.

Preheat the oven to 450°F.

Press the dough into a large rectangle on a work surface with your hands. Lift the dough and hold it by the top edge, allowing the weight of the dough to begin stretching it. Run your hands around the square as if you are turning a steering wheel, letting the dough weight stretch itself. Continue stretching the dough in the air or by pressing on the work surface until it is very thin. Transfer to a rimless baking sheet or the inverted side of a rimmed sheet pan and continue pressing and stretching until the dough is roughly a 9 × 15-inch rectangle, about 1/8-inch thick. The dough may stick to the sheet pan, but it will help the flatbread keep its shape while it bakes.

Brush the surface of the dough with 2 to 3 tablespoons garlic olive oil and prick it all over with a fork.

In a small bowl, mix the ricotta, chopped rosemary, and 1/2 teaspoon garlic olive oil until combined; season with salt and pepper and mix well. With a small spatula or spoon, spread a thin, even layer of the ricotta over the surface of the dough, leaving a 1/4-inch border. Scatter the quartered figs evenly over the surface. Transfer the flatbread to the oven and bake until edges are golden brown and dough is crisp, 15 to 18 minutes.

Remove from the oven and carefully run a thin icing spatula under the flatbread to release it from the pan if it is stuck. Transfer it to a cutting board and cut into squares or rectangles. Transfer to a serving platter, drizzle with a little garlic olive oil, and sprinkle more chopped rosemary over the top, if desired. Serve immediately.

STEAMED ARTICHOKES with HERBED YOGURT

4 large artichokes, rinsed

1 teaspoon sea salt plus more as needed

1 tablespoon black peppercorns

Zest and juice of 1 lemon

1 clove garlic

1 cup Greek yogurt or unsalted butter

2 tablespoons chopped fresh basil

Freshly cracked pepper, to taste

YIELD: 4 SERVINGS

What makes this recipe really sing:
My mom use to steam artichokes as a snack for my brother and me and I still get excited when I eat this forgotten treat. They are healthy yet buttery soft and so much fun to serve as an appetizer. Each person gets to slowly enjoy a whole artichoke, leaf by leaf, and end the pleasurable experience with that gorgeous golden heart.

What to toss in if you have it:
I love the taste of tart yogurt with the artichoke leaves. You can add spices like cumin and coriander to jazz up the yogurt dip or, for real traditional decadence, melt a stick of butter and add some minced garlic and the juice of half a lemon to dip the leaves into. Tarragon marries well with these flavors too; swap it for the basil if it's a fave flavor.

To prepare the artichokes, trim the stems, leaving about ½ inch, and remove the darker small leaves from the bottoms. Cut ½ to 1 inch off the top of each artichoke and, using kitchen scissors, trim the pointed tips off the remaining leaves.

Stand the trimmed artichokes upright in deep saucepan large enough to hold all four securely. Pour in approximately 3 inches very hot tap water, sea salt, peppercorns, lemon zest, and lemon juice. Bring the liquid to a simmer, cover, and cook until the stem ends of the artichokes have no resistance when pierced with a fork, 35 to 40 minutes. Remove the artichokes and drain them by turning them upside down on a plate and let them stand until cool enough to handle.

Meanwhile, put the garlic on a cutting board, sprinkle with a pinch of salt, and mash it into a paste with the back of a knife. Stir it into the yogurt along with the basil; season with salt and pepper.

Serve the artichokes with bowls of the herb yogurt to dip into and bowls for the discarded leaves.

ROASTED JALAPEÑO EGG ROLLS

Roast the jalapeños by holding them over a gas flame burner with tongs, turning them until blackened all over, or by putting them on a baking sheet and broiling them, turning as necessary, until blackened on all sides. Put the peppers into a plastic bag and seal it shut; this will steam the skin and make them easy to peel. Remove the skins by rubbing with a paper towel; cut a slit in one side of each pepper and pull out the membrane and seeds and discard. Remove the stems.

In a small bowl, mash the cream cheese and corn together and season with salt and pepper. Using a small spoon, fill each pepper cavity with a tablespoon of the corn mixture and enclose the filling inside the pepper, re-forming it into its natural shape. Lay a wonton skin on a work surface and lay a stuffed jalapeño across one corner. Roll the pepper in the wrapper halfway, and then fold in the corners. Use your finger to brush a little water along the exposed edge of the wonton skin and wrap the pepper up completely. Repeat with the remaining peppers and wonton skins. Cover the egg rolls with plastic wrap and refrigerate for at least 30 minutes.

Fill a small pot with corn oil to a depth of 2 inches and heat it over medium high to 375°F. Working in batches, deep-fry the egg rolls, turning them, until golden brown and crisp, about 4 minutes total. Drain them on a paper towel–lined plate and be sure to let the oil come back up to temperature before frying more.

Serve the egg rolls warm with your favorite salsa to dip them in.

12 large jalapeños

2 ounces cream cheese, at room temperature

½ cup cooked corn kernels

Kosher salt and freshly cracked black pepper, to taste

12 wonton wrappers

Corn or vegetable oil, for frying

YIELD: 6 SERVINGS

What makes this recipe really sing:
This is a fun spin on jalapeño poppers, but in the form of an egg roll. I love the creamy texture of warm cream cheese inside—and the wonton skin is super crunchy.

What to toss in if you have it:
You can make these really gooey inside by adding some finely grated Jack or Chihuahua cheese to the filling. Some finely diced cooked shrimp would be great in the filling as well, or try laying a slice of avocado next to the pepper inside the wonton. Fried avocado gets super soft and silky and tastes amazing.

MEXICAN SHRIMP COCKTAIL

2 limes, divided, plus more as needed

10 black peppercorns

1 pound jumbo shrimp, peeled, deveined, and tails left on

6 dried chiles de arbol

4 garlic cloves, skin on

6 large tomatoes

Kosher salt and freshly cracked black pepper, to taste

YIELD: 6 TO 8 SERVINGS

What makes this recipe really sing:
My friends, Shannon and Octavio, made a unique shrimp cocktail for me and I just had to know what was in it right away! It was so fresh and flavorful. Together we all pulled the five most prominent flavors and made it again. It is now our tradition to share this when we get together!

What to toss in if you have it:
Boil shrimp in beer and add a bay leaf. I love to serve this with my Cucumber-Watermelon Margarita (page 53).

Bring a large pot of water to a boil; squeeze the juice of 1 lime into the water and toss in the squeezed halves along with the peppercorns. Simmer for a few minutes and then drop in the shrimp. Reduce the heat to maintain a gentle simmer and cook until the shrimp are opaque but not overcooked, about 3 minutes. Drain the shrimp and run them under cool water. Squeeze the juice of ½ lime over them and refrigerate until cold.

Heat a large cast-iron skillet or griddle over medium high heat. Put the chiles on the hot dry skillet and toast them, turning frequently, until they darken a bit, just a minute or two. Do not overtoast or they will become bitter. Put the chiles in a bowl and cover them with hot water; let them stand until softened, about 10 minutes.

Put the garlic cloves in their skins on the skillet and toast them, turning occasionally until they are blackened and soft, about 10 minutes. Set the tomatoes on the skillet also and let them blacken, turning occasionally, until most of the sides are scorched. (Don't worry if the peel sticks to the skillet—the tomatoes are still drawing in smoky flavor.)

Drain the chiles, remove the stems, and put them into the bowl of a food processor. Peel the garlic cloves and add them; coarsely chop the blackened tomatoes and put them in the processor as well. Squeeze the juice of the remaining ½ lime into the bowl, then pulse the ingredients until a thick sauce forms. Season the sauce with salt and pepper and add more lime juice if necessary.

To serve, transfer the sauce to a bowl and drape the ice-cold poached shrimp over the rim of the bowl.

4.

ALL DAY EATS

SOUPS AND SALADS TO TIDE YOU OVER

I have a rocky relationship with soups and salads:
I always give them a shot, but I'm usually left
feeling cheated out of a real, full meal. That's
why I've worked hard to find these stand-alone
staples that are good enough to satisfy even
the toughest of critics. With dishes like Zucchini
Ribbon Salad or Curried Sugar Pumpkin Soup,
there's a perfect harmony of flavors and every
bite feels complex and delicious. Once you find
that soup or salad you love, you will return to it
again and again.

ROASTED BEETS with ORANGES and GOAT CHEESE

2 large red beets (about 1 pound), scrubbed

1 1/2 teaspoons lemon-flavored olive oil plus more as needed

1 navel orange

4 ounces goat cheese

Kosher salt and freshly cracked black pepper, to taste

1/3 cup dried cranberries, chopped

YIELD: 4 SERVINGS

What makes this recipe really sing:
Beets and goat cheese are now a classic combination thanks to this type of salad on so many restaurant menus. The mineral flavor of red beets and sweet cranberries is a surprisingly good combination. Lemon oil and orange segments round out the dish.

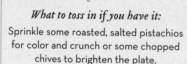

What to toss in if you have it:
Sprinkle some roasted, salted pistachios for color and crunch or some chopped chives to brighten the plate.

Preheat the oven to 375°F.

Put the beets on a piece of aluminum foil; drizzle with lemon olive oil and wrap them tightly. Transfer the foil packet to a baking sheet and roast until the beets are soft and a knife inserted in them meets no resistance, 1 to 1¼ hours. Cool to room temperature.

Meanwhile, zest the orange and reserve. Using a sharp knife, cut away the orange pith and remove the orange segments by cutting them away from the membrane. Squeeze the membrane over a bowl to catch the juice and chop the orange into small pieces.

Put the goat cheese in a small bowl, stir in ½ teaspoon zest, ½ teaspoon orange juice, and 1 teaspoon lemon olive oil. Season with salt and pepper and mix well.

Using a paper towel, rub the peels off the cooled beets. Grate the beets on the large holes of a box grater set over a bowl. Add the cranberries, chopped orange segments, and ½ teaspoon lemon olive oil; season with salt and pepper and stir well to combine.

To assemble, put a 3-inch round cookie cutter or ring mold on a salad plate. Fill with ¼ of the beet mixture, pressing lightly to pack it into the ring. Carefully pull the cookie cutter up and off the beets; repeat with remaining beet mixture on three more plates. Using two large spoons, form an oval-shaped ball with ¼ of the goat cheese mixture and gently rest it on the beets; repeat with remaining goat cheese. Drizzle the plates with lemon olive oil and garnish the cheese with any remaining orange zest. Serve at room temperature.

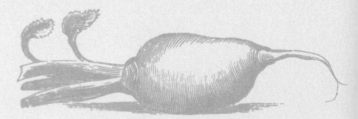

FENNEL, STRAWBERRY, and ARUGULA SALAD

Put the balsamic vinegar in a small saucepan, season with salt and pepper, and bring to a simmer over medium-high heat. Cook until the vinegar is reduced to about ⅓ cup and syrupy, about 15 minutes; cool to room temperature.

Remove the feathery fronds from the fennel bulb and reserve. Remove the core from the fennel and, using a mandoline or a knife, shave the fennel into very thin slices. Transfer them to a salad bowl along with the arugula and almonds. Drizzle the reduced vinegar over the greens, season with salt and pepper, and toss until coated. Sprinkle the strawberries and fennel fronds over the top of the salad and serve immediately.

1 cup white balsamic vinegar

Kosher salt and freshly ground black pepper, to taste

1 large fennel bulb with fronds

3 ounces (about 4 cups) baby arugula

¼ cup sliced almonds, toasted

1 pint fresh strawberries, hulled and quartered lengthwise

YIELD: 4 SERVINGS

What makes this recipe really sing:
White balsamic vinegar is sweeter than regular, but still has an acidic bite. By simmering it until it's thick and syruplike, it becomes concentrated in both tartness and sweetness. All you need to do is drizzle it over the salad—no dressing required!

What to toss in if you have it:
Slice some shallots or red onion paper thin with a mandoline and sprinkle some over the greens. Some crumbled, tart goat cheese over the top will add a creamy touch and is great with sweet strawberries and crunchy almonds.

ZUCCHINI RIBBON SALAD

Using a mandoline, cut the zucchini lengthwise into paper-thin ribbons and transfer to a fine-mesh strainer set over a bowl. Toss the zucchini with 2 tablespoons olive oil, season with salt and pepper, and let stand until the zucchini softens and releases excess liquid, about 10 minutes.

Meanwhile, heat 2 tablespoons olive oil in a small skillet over medium-high heat. Add the shallots, season with salt and pepper, and cook until light golden brown, about 5 minutes. Transfer the olive oil and shallots to a bowl. Add the fresh bread crumbs to the skillet and return to low heat. Add ½ teaspoon olive oil and toast the bread crumbs, stirring frequently until light golden brown; transfer to a small bowl and toss them with the lemon zest and some salt and pepper.

Add the lemon juice to the shallots and, while whisking, slowly drizzle in about 3 tablespoons olive oil until emulsified and thick; season with salt and pepper.

Transfer the drained zucchini to a serving platter, add ¼ cup toasted bread crumbs and gently toss to combine. Drizzle the dressing evenly over the zucchini, season with salt and pepper, and sprinkle remaining bread crumbs over the top. Serve immediately.

2 small zucchini (about 1 pound), stemmed

5 ½ teaspoons extra-virgin olive oil, divided, plus more as needed

Kosher salt and freshly cracked black pepper, to taste

1 small shallot, finely chopped

1 cup fresh bread crumbs

Zest of 1 lemon plus juice of ½ lemon

YIELD: 4 TO 6 SERVINGS

What makes this recipe really sing:
Cooking the shallots until golden brown completely changes their flavor from onionlike to almost nutty. Add the toasted bread crumbs, and even a zucchini hater will like this dish.

What to toss in if you have it:
Stir some grated Parmesan into the cooled toasted bread crumbs before sprinkling them over the zucchini for an Italian twist.

LAYERED CRAB SALAD

8 ounces fresh lump crabmeat, picked over

1 tablespoon finely chopped chives, divided

2 1/2 teaspoons lemon-flavored olive oil, divided

Kosher salt and freshly cracked black pepper, to taste

2 medium vine-ripened tomatoes, seeded and finely diced

1 avocado, peeled, pitted, and cut into 1/4-inch dice

YIELD: 4 SERVINGS

What makes this recipe really sing:
This is a dish that's all about the best ingredients. Make sure you have perfectly ripe summer tomatoes, a soft avocado, and fresh ice-cold crabmeat. A drizzle of lemony olive oil is all you need for a refreshing first course.

What to toss in if you have it:
These ingredients can be easily tossed gently together and served in butter lettuce leaves or piled on crostini as a fresh party hors d'oeuvre.

Put the crabmeat in a small bowl and gently toss it with 1 teaspoon chives, 1 teaspoon lemon olive oil, and salt and pepper until combined. In a second bowl, mix the tomatoes with 1/2 teaspoon lemon olive oil and salt and pepper. Put the diced avocado in a third bowl, add the remaining 1 teaspoon lemon olive oil, 1 teaspoon chives, salt and pepper, and toss well.

To assemble, divide 3/4 of the crab among four 6-ounce wide-rimmed glasses. Top the crab in each glass with 1/4 of the tomatoes, followed by 1/4 of the avocado. Use the remaining crabmeat to garnish each glass and sprinkle the remaining chives evenly over each salad. Serve immediately or chill and serve within an hour.

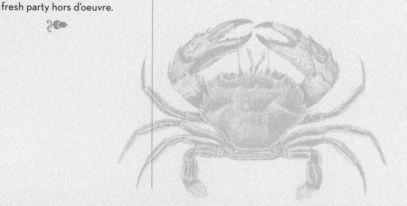

GRILLED ROMAINE SPEARS with CITRUS VINAIGRETTE

Preheat a grill pan over high heat.

Brush the romaine spears with lemon olive oil and season with salt and pepper. Place the spears on the grill pan and cook, turning once, until grill marks appear and lettuce begins to wilt, about 2 minutes total.

With a sharp knife, cut the peel and pith from the orange. Carefully remove the orange segments by cutting them lengthwise away from the membrane; transfer the segments to a cutting board, chop them, and reserve. Squeeze the membrane over a small bowl to catch the juice; while whisking, slowly drizzle in 2 tablespoons lemon olive oil until combined. Season with salt and pepper; add the chopped orange and shallots and stir to combine.

To serve, arrange the grilled romaine spears on a platter and drizzle the citrus vinaigrette over them.

2 romaine hearts, halved lengthwise through the core

Lemon-flavored olive oil

1 navel orange

½ small shallot, minced (about 2 teaspoons)

1 teaspoon Dijon mustard

Kosher salt and freshly cracked black pepper, to taste

YIELD: 4 SERVINGS

What makes this recipe really sing:
It may seem strange to grill salad, but romaine is sturdy and firm and stands up well to the heat. The leaves take on a smoky flavor and still have some crunch. The sweet orange and the bite of shallots make a very memorable salad.

What to toss in if you have it:
Marinate some jumbo shrimp in orange juice and grill them with the romaine. Serve them atop the smoky spears of lettuce for a terrific summer lunch.

SWEET and SPICY GRILLED HALLOUMI SALAD

One 4-ounce block halloumi cheese, halved horizontally

2 tablespoons garlic-chili-flavored olive oil plus more as needed

1 small cubanelle (Italian pepper)

1 tablespoon honey

Kosher salt and freshly ground black pepper, to taste

4 ounces baby arugula or mâche, for serving

YIELD: 4 SERVINGS

What makes this recipe really sing:
Halloumi, what I like to call "squeaky cheese," is a super firm Greek cheese made from a mixture of sheep and goat's milk. Its texture can stand up to searing and grilling without melting. Think of feta, but chewier; the spicy garlic-chili olive oil, sweet honey, and bright crunch of the peppers make this a fantastically well-rounded dish.

What to toss in if you have it:
Marinate some large shrimp in lemon and olive oil and grill them along with the cheese; this salad/appetizer with shrimp or even a piece of fresh grilled fish would make a terrific lunch or light summer supper.

Heat a gas grill to high heat or a stovetop grill pan to high.

Put the cheese on a plate and drizzle some garlic-chili olive oil over the surface, rubbing the pieces together to coat in oil. Using a metal spatula, transfer the oiled cheese to the hot grill and cook just until deep grill marks appear and the cheese releases itself from the grate or grill pan, 3 to 4 minutes. Carefully flip it and grill on the opposite side until grill marks appear, about 3 minutes more. Transfer it to a cutting board and cool slightly. Cut it into thin strips.

Meanwhile, put the pepper on the grill and cook, turning frequently, until lightly charred. Let stand until cool enough to handle and remove the stem and seeds from the pepper; cut into a small dice and reserve.

In a small bowl, whisk together 2 tablespoons garlic-chili olive oil and honey until the honey has dissolved. Season the mixture with salt and pepper and stir in the diced peppers.

To serve, put a small pile of greens on four appetizer plates. Arrange the cheese strips on each plate, and then drizzle ¼ of the peppers and honey vinaigrette over the halloumi. Season the cheese and greens with salt and pepper and serve immediately.

BACON and EGG SALAD

6 ounces slab bacon, cut into
½-inch pieces

1 shallot, minced

6 cups water

3 tablespoons champagne vinegar,
divided

4 large fresh farm eggs

½ pound frisée (about 2 large
heads), washed, dried, and
chopped into bite-size pieces

Kosher salt and freshly cracked
black pepper, to taste

YIELD: 4 SERVINGS

What makes this recipe really sing:
This classic French bistro salad is one
of my absolute favorites. If you've
never had it, it may sound like a strange
combination, but it is just delicious.
Sweet shallots, tart vinegar, salty bacon
drippings, creamy egg yolk, crunchy
bacon, soft poached egg white, crisp tart
frisée—it's perfection on a plate.

What to toss in if you have it:
This salad is incredible as is, but if
you have other hearty greens like
wild arugula, toss them in with the mix.
The warm dressing will wilt them
lightly, so use firm greens for this. You
can also slice and dust more shallots
in flour, then shallow fry them until
crisp and sprinkle them over the top for
another crisp onion crunch.

Cook the bacon pieces in a large skillet over medium-high heat until crisp; transfer to a paper towel–lined plate to drain. Add the shallot to the skillet and cook until softened, 2 to 3 minutes. Pour in 2 tablespoons vinegar, reduce the heat, and simmer gently for a minute.

In another skillet or low saucepan, bring the water and 1 tablespoon vinegar to a gentle simmer. Crack an egg into a small bowl and gently slip it into the water, swirling the water gently around the egg with a spoon to surround the yolk with egg white. Cook until the white is set but the yolk is still runny, 1½ to 2 minutes. Repeat with the remaining eggs.

Add the frisée and crisp bacon pieces to the warm pan dressing, season with salt and pepper, and toss to coat.

Divide the dressed frisée and bacon among four plates; top with a poached egg and season with salt and pepper. Serve immediately.

ROASTED TOMATO–BREAD SOUP

Preheat the oven to 400°F.

Place the fresh tomatoes on a rimmed baking sheet and toss with 2 tablespoons garlic olive oil and season with salt and pepper. Roast in the oven for 15 minutes.

Meanwhile, heat 1 tablespoon garlic olive oil in a saucepan over medium high heat. Add the basil and stir for about 30 seconds. Add the canned tomatoes with their juice and the water; season with salt and pepper. Bring to a boil over medium-high heat, then reduce the heat to medium low and simmer 15 minutes. Stir in the bread and simmer 2 to 3 minutes.

Stir the oven-roasted tomatoes and any cooking juices into the saucepan; simmer for another 3 minutes. Taste for seasoning, adjusting if necessary, and ladle into bowls.

To serve, garnish with a drizzle of garlic olive oil and torn basil leaves.

Note: *If you don't have garlic olive oil, add 2 cloves of minced garlic to 3 tablespoons heated olive oil and sauté for 2 to 3 minutes.*

1 pound vine-ripened tomatoes, quartered and seeded

3 tablespoons garlic-infused extra-virgin olive oil plus more for garnish

Kosher salt and fresh finely ground black pepper, to taste

1/2 cup finely chopped fresh basil leaves plus more for garnish

One 28-ounce can crushed San Marzano tomatoes

1 1/2 cups water

3 cups day-old sourdough baguette or country bread, torn or cut into 1/2-inch cubes

YIELD: 4 TO 6 SERVINGS

What makes this recipe really sing:
You can enjoy this soup even when tomatoes aren't their best in the winter months by roasting them until concentrated and sweet. They get a boost with San Marzano tomatoes, which are hands down the best canned tomatoes available. This is incredibly filling soup—a meal in a bowl.

What to toss in if you have it:
Throw a couple of garlic cloves on the baking sheet with the tomatoes, then chop them and add them to the soup for sweet roasted garlic flavor.

POTATO BAR SOUP

4 strips smoky bacon

3 large leeks, woody green ends removed, sliced and rinsed

1 ½ pounds Yukon Gold potatoes, peeled and cut into 1-inch chunks

6 cups low-sodium chicken stock

Kosher salt and freshly ground black pepper, to taste

Grated cheddar cheese, for serving

YIELD: 6 SERVINGS

What makes this recipe really sing:
This is my tribute to those baked potato bars in diners and steakhouses in the '80s and '90s. Potatoes and leeks are a classic combination, but add some crunchy bacon and cheddar cheese and you have a loaded baked potato in a bowl!

What to toss in if you have it:
You can add anything to this soup you would add to a baked potato; some corn kernels or broccoli florets for example. Garnish the bowl with a dollop of sour cream and sprinkle some sliced scallions on top of that.

Put the bacon strips in a large Dutch oven or heavy soup pot and cook over medium heat until crisp, about 6 minutes. Transfer to a paper towel–lined plate to drain; reserve. Add the leeks to the bacon drippings and cook, stirring, until softened and light golden brown, about 10 minutes. Using a slotted spoon, remove the cooked leeks and set aside.

Add the potatoes and chicken stock to the pot. Add salt and a healthy grind of black pepper and bring the mixture to a simmer. Cover, reduce the heat to medium low, and cook until the potatoes are fork tender but still holding their shape, 12 to 15 minutes. With the slotted spoon, remove about 2 cups of the potatoes and transfer them to a food processor or blender; add about 1 cup chicken stock and pulse the potatoes until broken down. Do not overmix—add more liquid if necessary to get them moving in the machine, but stop when they are liquefied. Pour the potato puree back into the pot and stir in the browned leeks. Taste and adjust the seasoning.

To serve, ladle the hot soup into warm bowls, crumble some bacon over the top along with a little grated cheese.

SPANISH GAZPACHO

Soak the bread in water until soft, about 2 minutes. Squeeze out water for bread to resemble a dough-like consistency.

Remove skins from tomatoes by bringing a large pot of water to a boil. Cut a shallow "×" on the top of each tomato and drop in the boiling water for 60 seconds to blanche. Meanwhile, prepare an ice bath by filling a large bowl with ice and water. Remove blanched tomatoes from boiling water and immediately plunge tomatoes into ice bath. Remove skins of tomatoes and quarter, removing seeds.

In a food processor or blender, blend bread and almonds until almonds are finely chopped. While motor is running, add oil in a slow, steady stream. Once a smooth, thick consistency is reached, add in skinned and seeded tomatoes and the vinegar. Season to taste with salt and pepper and blend until smooth. Refrigerate soup for at least one hour.

Serve this rich soup chilled, in small portions, with crusty bread and enjoy!

One 4-inch crustless baguette (reserve remaining baguette for serving)

1/2 cup water

2 pounds ripe tomatoes

1/4 cup whole blanched almonds

1 cup garlic-infused olive oil

2 tablespoons sherry vinegar

Kosher salt and freshly cracked black pepper, to taste

YIELD: 4 TO 6 SERVINGS

What makes this recipe really sing:
I especially love the Spanish flair of this cold soup and how incredible the consistency is; it's almost like a sauce and could even be great served as a dip for cold seafood. Be sure to make this when tomatoes are at their peak of ripeness and use a good sherry vinegar, such as a reserva. Try using Marcona almonds if you have them; they are extra buttery and a bit of an indulgence in this soup.

What to toss in if you have it:
Finely chopped hard-boiled egg and thin slices of Serrano ham are classic garnishes for this soup. I personally love to add just the ham and I usually fry julienned strips in a bit of olive oil to crisp before topping the cold soup. It's incredibly yummy!

CREAMY GRILLED CORN SOUP

Preheat a grill pan or gas grill to medium-high.

Grill the corn, turning frequently, until lightly charred all over, about 10 minutes. With a sharp knife, cut the kernels from the cobs; reserve ½ cup for garnish and put the rest in a bowl. Put 2 of the cobs back on the grill and cook, turning, until lightly charred. With the back of the knife, scrape all the cobs firmly to extract the milky liquid and add it to the kernels in the bowl. Break the 2 grilled cobs into pieces and set aside.

Melt the butter in a large saucepan over medium heat. Add the onion and cook, stirring, until softened and translucent, about 5 minutes. Season with salt and pepper; add the vegetable stock, corn kernels, milky liquid, and grilled cob pieces to the pan (this will add smoky flavor to the soup). Bring the mixture to a boil, cover, and reduce the heat to maintain a simmer. Cook until the corn and onion are very soft, about 15 minutes. Remove the grilled cob pieces from the pot and discard. Working in small batches, puree the mixture in a blender and transfer to a clean saucepan. Add the half-and-half and warm the soup gently over medium-low heat; if it is too thick, add a bit more half-and-half to reach the desired consistency. Taste and adjust the seasoning.

Serve the hot soup in warm bowls with some grilled corn kernels scattered over the top.

4 fresh large sweet corn cobs, husks and silk removed

3 tablespoons unsalted butter

1 yellow onion, chopped

Kosher salt and freshly ground black pepper, to taste

3 cups vegetable stock

1 cup half-and-half plus more as needed

YIELD: 4 TO 6 SERVINGS

What makes this recipe really sing:
Grilling the cobs after removing the kernels and cooking them with the soup adds an even deeper smoky flavor; it's rich and satisfying and not nearly as heavy as corn chowder. It's like making stock with chicken bones— you pull every ounce of flavor out of the ingredient you can.

What to toss in if you have it:
To bulk this soup up, add diced red potatoes and sliced celery after you puree it and simmer gently until the potatoes are cooked. Some leftover pulled chicken meat will turn this soup into a one-pot meal.

CURRIED SUGAR PUMPKIN SOUP

One 3-pound sugar pumpkin

2 tablespoons extra-virgin olive oil plus more for roasting

Kosher salt and freshly cracked black pepper, to taste

2 shallots, chopped

1 quart low-sodium chicken stock

2 teaspoons curry powder (mild or spicy)

YIELD: 4 TO 6 SERVINGS

What makes this recipe really sing:
Sugar pumpkins have much more flavor than the plain old jack-o'-lantern type. They are small and cute, usually weighing about 3 pounds, and when roasted are sweet as candy. The flesh makes a terrific soup, especially when mixed with warming curry.

What to toss in if you have it:
Although this soup is hearty, delicious, and very healthy, a little half-and-half or heavy cream will make it rich and smooth. For a pretty presentation, drizzle some thinned crème fraîche over the soup in each bowl and sprinkle some toasted sliced almonds for a little crunch.

Preheat the oven to 375°F.

Cut the pumpkin in half through the stem and remove the seeds. Drizzle the cut edges with olive oil, season with salt and pepper, and put cut side down on a baking sheet. Roast until very soft, about 45 minutes. Remove from the oven, turn the halves over, and let them stand until cool enough to handle. Scoop the flesh from the shells, transfer to a bowl, and discard the shells.

In a large saucepan or Dutch oven with a lid, heat the 2 tablespoons olive oil over medium heat. Add the shallots and cook until softened, about 6 minutes. Add the pumpkin flesh, chicken stock, and curry powder and bring to a boil. Reduce the heat to maintain a simmer, cover, and cook until pumpkin is broken down, about 10 minutes.

Working in batches, puree the soup in a blender until smooth or use a blender wand, transferring the puree to a clean saucepan as you work. Season the soup with salt and pepper and simmer a few minutes over medium heat to marry the flavors. Serve immediately.

SPICY COCONUT CHICKEN SOUP

4 large skin-on, bone-in chicken breast halves

3 quarts water

1 teaspoon black peppercorns

6 scallions, divided

2 limes

Two 14-ounce cans coconut milk

2 teaspoons sriracha or sambal, or to taste

Kosher salt and freshly cracked black pepper, to taste

YIELD: 4 TO 6 SERVINGS

What makes this recipe really sing:
Whenever you can make your own chicken stock, do it. You can flavor your stock anyway you like, and you can be sure you are using the best ingredients. The stock base for this soup is bright and acidic, which is mellowed by the fatty richness of the coconut milk.

What to toss in if you have it:
Add a few sprigs of cilantro to the stock for a true Asian flavor; float some cilantro leaves in the soup along with some enoki or sautéed shiitake mushrooms for a fantastic first course.

Put the chicken, water, peppercorns, and 4 whole scallions in a large saucepan or stockpot. Halve the limes, squeeze the juice from them into the pot, and add the squeezed halves. Bring to a simmer slowly over medium heat. Cover and cook 45 minutes, until chicken is cooked through and falling from the bone.

With tongs, remove the chicken from the pan and let stand until cool enough to handle. Remove the skin and pull the chicken meat into strands with a fork; reserve and discard the bones and skin. Strain the stock through a fine-mesh strainer into a large bowl, discarding the solids. The stock can be refrigerated once at room temperature and the solidified fat skimmed from the surface, if desired.

To make the soup, put 1 quart stock into a saucepan. Add the coconut milk and sriracha and bring to a gentle simmer. Add the pulled chicken meat; and season with salt and pepper. Just before serving, slice the remaining scallions and add them to the soup.

Note: *Any leftover stock can be frozen up to 1 month and used for soups whenever chicken broth is called for.*

LEMON-TARRAGON CHICKEN SOUP

Preheat oven to 400°F.

Put the garlic halves cut side down on a sheet of aluminum foil on a rimmed baking sheet. Add 2 tablespoons chicken stock and wrap the foil around garlic, keeping the cut sides flat on the baking sheet. Transfer to the oven and roast about 30 minutes, until the garlic is very soft. Remove from the oven and let stand until cool enough to handle.

Squeeze the soft garlic from the halves with your fingers into a large saucepan. Whisk in 1 cup stock to loosen the garlic paste and put the pan over medium-high heat. Add the remaining stock, lemon juice, and chopped tarragon; season with salt and pepper. Bring the mixture to a boil, reduce to a simmer, and add the chicken; Cover and cook until the chicken is just cooked through, 9 to 12 minutes.

Ladle the soup into bowls and garnish with thin lemon slices and a sprinkle of fresh tarragon leaves.

1 large garlic head, cut in half horizontally through the cloves

4 cups low-sodium chicken stock

1/2 cup freshly squeezed lemon juice plus 1 lemon thinly sliced, for garnish

2 tablespoons chopped fresh tarragon plus more tarragon, for garnish

Sea salt and freshly cracked black pepper, to taste

2 skinless, boneless chicken breasts, preferably organic, cut into bite-size pieces

YIELD: 4 TO 6 SERVINGS

What makes this recipe really sing:
If you like garlic, you'll love this soup. This should cure any cold! Roasting the garlic mellows the flavor, and the lemon juice and tarragon give the soup some brightness. Free-range or organic chicken is a must here—it is much juicier and flavorful than the mass-produced chicken found in most grocery stores.

What to toss in if you have it:
You can add just about any vegetable to the soup; chicken breast cooks quickly, so there are no worries about overcooking vegetables in the broth. Broccoli, peas, fresh corn kernels, celery, and carrots would all be great additions.

5.

The
MAIN EVENT

IMPRESSIVE ENTRÉES

Here's where you get to show off your cooking chops and let your main ingredient shine. You don't need many add-ons when you're working with a beautiful piece of fish or an organic chicken breast. No matter the audience or occasion—a holiday party, family supper, or a summer barbecue—these main dishes are the hearty cornerstone of any meal.

DRY-RUBBED BBQ CHICKEN

In a large plastic container with a lid, add 8 cups water, ¾ cup salt, ¾ cup brown sugar, the vinegar, and 1 tablespoon BBQ seasoning. Stir until well mixed. Add the chicken to brine and refrigerate at least 2 hours and no longer than 4.

Preheat the oven to 350°F.

Remove the chicken from the brine and pat dry. Make a spice rub with 1 teaspoon salt, 1 tablespoon brown sugar and 2 tablespoons BBQ seasoning mix. Rub the outside of the chicken with spice rub and place in a roasting pan. Add 2 tablespoons water to the bottom of the pan and place in the oven. Roast for 45 minutes, or until the internal temperature at the thickest point of the meat reaches 160°F. Allow the chicken to rest for 5 minutes loosely covered with foil before carving.

8 cups plus 2 tablespoons water

¾ cup plus 1 teaspoon kosher salt

¾ cup plus 1 tablespoon light brown sugar

¾ cup white vinegar

3 tablespoons dry BBQ seasoning mix, divided

2 large skin-on, bone-in chicken breast halves

YIELD: 4 SERVINGS

What makes this recipe really sing:
Soaking the chicken in a sweet and salty brine and coating it with a dry rub gives it a rich smoky flavor without the mess of charcoal. It is scientifically proven that the correct levels of salt in the brine actually swell the cells of the meat, allowing it to absorb more moisture and be much juicier. Foolproof!

What to toss in if you have it:
Brines for poultry can be flavored in a myriad of ways. Squeeze the juice of a navel orange into it along with the peels and a few bay leaves for a more herbal, citrus flavor in the meat. The only thing missing in the recipe is a great BBQ sauce to slather over it. No fear—I have you covered! Try my super easy BBQ sauce recipe on page 114.

BBQ SAUCE

One 7-ounce jar or can organic tomato paste

3/4 cup packed dark brown sugar

3 tablespoons spicy Dijon mustard

2 tablespoons BBQ seasoning mix

2 tablespoons Worcestershire sauce

1 teaspoon kosher salt

1/2 teaspoon freshly cracked black pepper

4 cups water

YIELD: ABOUT 2 CUPS

What makes this recipe really sing:
Finding a great BBQ spice blend to keep in the pantry makes this dish so simple to whip together. Be sure to check the sodium content of spice blends when purchasing. I love to jar this sauce as a hostess gift for a summer weekend stay or when heading to a friend's outdoor party. A gift of homemade BBQ sauce is always a huge hit!

What to toss in if you have it:
Depending on the dinner's mood, I sometimes add a splash of bourbon to play up the sweet notes, a pinch of cayenne pepper to kick up the heat, just a bit of apple cider vinegar to balance out the flavors for pork, or a finely minced chipotle in adobo sauce when I'm craving a touch of smoky flavor. Any or all options are fun, but I must say this BBQ sauce with my favorite BBQ seasoning blend hits all the best notes without any additions.

Whisk all the ingredients together in a large saucepan and bring to a boil over medium-high heat. Reduce the heat to maintain a simmer and cook, stirring occasionally, until reduced by about half, or to desired thickness, about 1 hour.

Cool the sauce completely before transferring it to an airtight container; store in the refrigerator for 1 week or freeze for up to 6 months.

CORNISH HENS au VIN

Heat a Dutch oven over medium heat and add bacon; cook until bacon is browned and crisp and fat is rendered. Remove bacon to drain on a paper towel–lined plate.

Put the flour in a large bowl and season heavily with salt and pepper. Toss the hens in seasoned flour until coated, shaking off excess. Brown the hens on all sides in the bacon fat. Carefully add the wine, letting it bubble and release the browned bits on the pan. Add the water and garlic cloves and bring to a boil; reduce heat to a gentle simmer. Cover and braise until hens are cooked through, about 20 minutes.

Transfer the hens to a platter and cover with aluminum foil to keep warm. Continue simmering the liquid, uncovered, until thickened, about 10 minutes. Taste the gravy and season if necessary; nestle the hens in the gravy and simmer until heated through. Crumble the bacon over the top and serve immediately.

4 slices thick-cut bacon

1/2 cup unbleached all purpose flour

Kosher salt and freshly cracked black pepper, to taste

8 Cornish hens, about 1 pound each, rinsed and patted dry

2 cups dry white wine

1 cup water

3 garlic cloves

YIELD: 6 TO 8 SERVINGS

What makes this recipe really sing:
A spin on the French classic Coq au Vin, or "chicken with wine." Typically it's made with red wine, but the white wine really allows the Cornish hens to be tasted. Smoky bacon adds an incredible undertone to the flavors in this dish. The individual portion size of the Cornish hens makes this the perfect entertaining entrée.

What to toss in if you have it:
I sometimes replace the water with vegetable or chicken stock to give a stronger veggie role and add an even richer flavor combination. Of course a sprinkle of fresh herbs never hurts any dish. When I have it on hand, I toss in some fresh thyme or fresh chopped flat-leaf parsley for a splash of color and mild flavor.

BUTTERMILK PECAN CHICKEN

Four 8-ounce skinless, boneless chicken breasts

1 cup buttermilk

1 cup toasted pecans

1 cup panko (Japanese bread crumbs)

1/3 cup vegetable oil

Kosher salt and freshly ground black pepper, to taste

YIELD: 4 SERVINGS

What makes this recipe really sing:
Highly acidic buttermilk is a fantastic tenderizer; soak any chicken you plan to cook—whether fried, baked, or grilled—and you'll be amazed at how juicy and tender the meat becomes.

❧

What to toss in if you have it:
A couple splashes of your favorite hot sauce into the buttermilk marinade adds a pleasant heat to the chicken. Grated lemon zest stirred into the pecan and panko breading mixture will add a bright note to this deliciously crunchy chicken.

❧

Place each chicken breast between two pieces of plastic wrap and gently flatten it with a meat mallet or heavy, flat object to an even 1/3-inch thick.

Marinate the chicken in buttermilk for 1 hour in refrigerator.

In a food processor, pulse the pecans and panko together until fine. Transfer the mixture to a large rimmed dish.

Remove the marinated chicken breasts from the buttermilk and shake off any excess. Dip the chicken in the breading mixture, evenly coating both sides.

In a large nonstick skillet, heat the oil. Working in two batches, add the breaded chicken breasts and shallow fry 4 to 5 minutes on each side until golden in color. Remove them from oil and drain on a paper towel–lined plate; season with salt and pepper immediately and serve.

Note: *If you'd rather not fry the chicken breasts, place them on a lightly greased baking dish and bake them for 25 to 30 minutes in an oven that has been preheated to 375°F.*

This chicken tastes great with the Cheesy Penne on page 186.

SPICED STONE FRUIT CHUTNEY

1 ½ cup dried apricots, chopped

1 cup dried cherries, chopped

1 cup pomegranate juice

2 cups water

Small pinch of salt

2 chai spiced tea bags

1 cup pecans, toasted and chopped

YIELD: 6 TO 8 SERVINGS

What makes this recipe really sing:
This is truly one of my favorites! I adore cranberry sauce when it's flowing through the holiday season. I wanted to find a way to re-create that flavor anytime of year, and the dried fruits make that possible. This is wonderful to use as a topping for your favorite hot porridge, or you can punch up your breakfast yogurt with a spoonful. As I have been known to eat this straight up with a spoon, I feel there is no limit to the uses of this recipe. It's also my go-to recipe when looking to jar a homemade little something to take along for a weekend visit with a friend or as a dinner party gift to the host.

What to toss in if you have it:
I tossed in some chopped crystallized ginger for my friend April because she adores ginger and it turned out great. I swap toasted walnuts or almonds sometimes for the pecans. Dried cranberries can certainly replace the cherries if desired.

Put the fruit into a medium heavy-bottomed pot over medium heat. Add pomegranate juice, water, and salt and bring to a simmer. Add the tea bags and simmer for about 40 minutes, until liquid has been mostly absorbed.

Remove the tea bags and discard; stir in the pecans and serve warm or at room temperature. Serve about ½ cup per person and enjoy!

ROASTED TURKEY BREAST with GRAVY

Preheat the oven to 375°F.

Dry the skin of the turkey breasts with paper towels and place meat side up on a roasting rack in a roasting pan. Rub 4 tablespoons butter all over the surface of each breast; season well with salt and pepper. Add the shallots to the bottom of the roasting pan and cover the shallots with the stock. Place the pan in the oven and roast until a meat thermometer registers 165°F and the juices run clear, about 1 hour (begin checking internal temperature after 45 minutes to prevent overcooking). Remove from the oven and place on a cutting board tented with aluminum to allow the turkey breasts to rest while making the gravy.

Strain the pan drippings into a small saucepan and bring to a simmer. In a small bowl, with a fork, mash together the remaining 2 tablespoons butter and the flour until a paste forms; whisk into the simmering stock, season with salt and pepper, and cook until thickened.

Carve the turkey breast meat from the bone and slice. Serve with gravy on the side.

Note: *If you're using a whole turkey, tuck the wings back. Adjust the temperature to 325°F and cook until a meat thermometer reaches 165°F in the breast and 180°F deep in the thigh meat. Loosely cover with foil if the breasts are browning too much. Allow them to rest, slightly covered, approximately 30 minutes before carving.*

Two 3-pound fresh skin-on, bone-in turkey breast halves

1/4 pound (1 stick) plus 2 tablespoons butter, at room temperature

Kosher salt and freshly cracked black pepper, to taste

2 shallots, peeled and sliced

2 cups good-quality low-sodium chicken stock

2 tablespoons unbleached all-purpose flour

YIELD: 6 TO 8 SERVINGS

What makes this recipe really sing:
This is Thanksgiving at its absolute simplest. Roasting just the breast on the bone takes a third the time a whole bird takes and removes that nervous stress of wondering whether that turkey is really cooked all the way through or not. Make it easy on yourself and spend more time on side dishes. This recipe is so simple and quick you can have turkey and gravy any night of the week.

What to toss in if you have it:
The butter can be flavored with chopped herbs, citrus zest, or minced garlic. You can also add some celery stalks and carrots to the roasting pan to give the gravy more flavor.

GINGER and LEMON ROASTED CHICKEN with BRAISED FENNEL

1 organic roasting chicken
(about 4 pounds)

One 6-inch piece fresh
ginger, peeled

6 tablespoons unsalted butter, at
room temperature, divided

Zest of 1 lemon, juice of ½ lemon,
and slices of ½ lemon for garnish

Kosher salt and freshly cracked
black pepper, to taste

2 whole fennel bulbs, with fronds

1 cup water

YIELD: 4 TO 6 SERVINGS

What makes this recipe really sing:
Ginger and chicken are usually combined
in Asian dishes, but I decided
I would take probably my favorite
ingredient and see what I could do with
a whole roasted bird. The spicy,
tangy ginger flavor permeates the
chicken and flavors the sweet fennel.
What a great combination!

What to toss in if you have it:
Grate a couple of garlic cloves and stir
them into the compound butter
before spreading it all over the bird,
and add some carrots and celery
to the roasting pan for a colorful side
dish with the braised fennel.

Remove the chicken from refrigerator and let stand at room temperature for 20 minutes. Preheat the oven to 425°F.

Cut off a 1-inch piece of ginger, grate it on a microplane, and transfer it to a bowl with 4 tablespoons butter. Add the lemon zest. Halve the lemon and squeeze the juice from ½ into the butter; slice the other half for garnish and reserve. Season the butter with salt and pepper and mix well.

Place the chicken on a roasting rack in a roasting pan. Loosen the skin of the chicken with your fingers under breast and down the thighs. Stuff the ginger-lemon butter under the skin and, using your fingers, spread the paste evenly over the breast meat and the thighs. Rub the exterior of the chicken with the remaining butter and season generously with salt and pepper. Remove the fronds from the fennel and reserve; trim the stalks from the bulbs and stuff them into the cavity of the chicken. Cut the bulbs into ¼-inch wedges and reserve. Using kitchen twine, tie the chicken legs to enclose the cavity.

Roast the chicken 20 minutes; remove the pan from the oven and reduce the heat to 375°F. Slice the remaining ginger into chunks and add to the roasting pan along with the fennel wedges and lemon slices. Pour in 1 cup water and return the pan to the oven and continue roasting until internal temperature registers 170°F, or until the juices run clear when the chicken is pierced with a fork, about 1½ hours more.

To serve, scatter the roasted fennel and lemon slices around a serving platter, rest the roasted chicken on top of the vegetables, and garnish with the reserved fennel fronds. Carve tableside.

PORK ROAST with HARD CIDER GRAVY

Preheat the oven to 375°F.

Heat a large Dutch oven over medium heat; when it is hot, add 2 tablespoons butter. Season the pork generously with salt and pepper and sear it on all sides in the hot pot until golden brown; remove and set aside. Add the onion and apples to the pot, season with salt and pepper, and cook until they begin to caramelize; pour in the hard cider and scrape the brown bits off the bottom of the pot. Bring to a simmer and nestle the browned pork roast back in the pot. Cover with the lid and place in the oven to braise until the internal temperature reaches 145°F on a meat thermometer, 25 to 30 minutes.

Remove the pork roast from the pot and transfer it to a carving board; tent it with foil to keep it warm. Transfer the contents of the pot to a food processor or blender and puree; return the puree to the pot. Bring to a boil, season with salt and pepper, then reduce the heat to low; add more cider if the gravy is too thick. Add the remaining tablespoon cold butter, whisking constantly as it melts; remove from the heat when the gravy is smooth and shiny and the butter is completely melted.

Slice the pork loin roast and serve it with sauce.

This roast is wonderful with the Ricotta-Thyme Spaetzle on page 181.

---

2 tablespoons plus 1 tablespoon (cold) unsalted butter

One 2 ½-pound pork loin roast, trimmed and tied

Kosher salt and freshly cracked black pepper, to taste

1 onion, peeled and sliced

2 Granny Smith apples, cored and sliced

One 12-ounce bottle, hard cider plus more as needed

YIELD: 4 SERVINGS

What makes this recipe really sing:
Tart Granny Smith apples are magically turned into gravy in this classic autumn comfort food favorite. Adding hard cider gives the gravy some added richness and kick. Whenever you take the time to caramelize vegetables or fruit, you bring out even more of their flavor and sugar. The deeper browned the onion and apples get, the more rich and flavorful your gravy will be.

What to toss in if you have it:
Although this gravy is tart and delicious as is, a spoonful of coarse-ground mustard will add an even more complex kick. If you have some spicy applesauce lying around, try a little on the side. There's no such thing as gilding the lily here!

GRILLED FLANK STEAK
with SPICY CORN RELISH

3 fresh large sweet corn cobs, husks and silk removed

1 small jalapeño

Zest and juice of 1 lime

Kosher salt and freshly cracked black pepper, to taste

1 tablespoon chopped cilantro

1 1/2 pounds flank steak

YIELD: 4 TO 6 SERVINGS

What makes this recipe really sing:
Flank steak is the unsung hero of the kitchen—inexpensive, quick to cook, and able to feed a crowd. Bright, acidic lime juice and the charcoal grill flavor are a great match.

What to toss in if you have it:
Toss a few red onion slices on the grill pan and chop them up; stir them into the salad with some finely diced roasted red peppers and diced avocado for a killer southwestern salsa.

Using tongs, cook the corn over the burners of a gas stove, or broil under a broiler set on high until blackened, turning the cobs until evenly charred. Using a sharp knife, cut the kernels from the cobs and transfer them to a bowl. Repeat with the jalapeño; wrap the charred pepper in a paper towel and let stand a few minutes to steam the peel. Use the paper towel to rub the blackened skin from the pepper. Remove the stem and seeds from the pepper, finely chop it, and add it to the corn. Add the lime zest and juice, chopped cilantro, season with salt and pepper, and toss until well combined. Set aside while you grill the steak.

Heat a grill pan over high heat until smoking. Season the steak with salt and pepper and place on the pan. Grill until marks appear and the meat releases itself from the grill, 3 to 4 minutes. Flip the steak and continue grilling 2 to 3 minutes for medium rare. Remove the steak and let it stand 10 minutes before thinly slicing it on the diagonal.

Serve the sliced flank steak with corn relish spooned over the top.

RIB EYE STEAKS au POIVRE

Preheat the oven to 375°F.

Heat a large, well-seasoned cast-iron skillet over high heat. Pat the steaks dry with a paper towel and season with salt; press 2 tablespoons pepper into the meat. Put the steaks into the hot skillet and cook until blackened and they have released themselves from the skillet. Turn the steaks and transfer the skillet to the oven. Cook until a meat thermometer reads 125°F for medium rare, or to desired doneness.

Remove the skillet from the oven and transfer the steaks to a cutting board; cover with aluminum foil to keep warm. Put the skillet back over medium heat. Carefully add the brandy and ignite it to burn off the alcohol. Add the cream, vinegar, and peppercorns and simmer until very thick. Stir in the butter just before serving.

Slice the steaks and serve them with peppercorn sauce.

2 bone-in rib eye steaks (about 1 1/2 pounds each)

Kosher salt, to taste

2 tablespoons coarsely cracked black pepper

1/2 cup brandy

1/2 cup heavy cream

2 tablespoons sherry vinegar

1 teaspoon coarsely crushed black peppercorns

2 tablespoons unsalted butter

YIELD: 4 SERVINGS

What makes this recipe really sing:
Anytime you can make a sauce from pan drippings, go for it. Rib eye steaks are well-marbled and the fat and juice they release have loads of flavor; don't waste them!

What to toss in if you have it:
If you really love pepper, this is the dish for you. In fact, if you have tricolored peppercorns, coarsely crush them and add them into the sauce. Red and green peppercorns have a much different flavor than black peppercorns. (Green peppercorns, or baby black peppercorns, are immature and a bit fresher with a sharp flavor. Red peppercorns are actually a dried berry from the Baie rose plant. They are slightly floral and have an almost citrus-zest flavor. I love them with grilled fruits, such as any melon or stone fruit.)

BEEF STEW– STUFFED POTATOES

8 cups low-sodium beef stock

3 large russet potatoes

5 tablespoons extra-virgin olive oil, divided

2 pounds beef chuck, trimmed and cut into 1-inch cubes

Kosher salt and freshly cracked black pepper, to taste

Water as needed

1 ½ cups frozen pearl onions

YIELD: 6 SERVINGS

What makes this recipe really sing:
It's virtually impossible to screw up braised stews and meats provided the meat is browned properly and cooked long enough. Reducing the beef stock in this recipe gives you instant gravy, and the mix of onions, tender beef, and crunchy potatoes is fantastic.

What to toss in if you have it:
The sky's the limit here; add any vegetable you enjoy in stews—carrots, celery, parsnips, or peas. For extra-rich sauce for the potato to soak up, add a bottle of dark beer to the braising liquid.

Preheat the oven to 400°F.

Pour the beef stock into a large saucepan and bring to a boil. Cook until the liquid is reduced by half, leaving 4 cups.

Put the potatoes on a rimmed baking sheet and roast until just tender, about 45 minutes. When they're cool enough to handle, cut the potatoes in half lengthwise and, using a spoon, remove the potato flesh and reserve, leaving a ½-inch-thick rim around the edges. Drizzle 1 tablespoon olive oil on the baking sheet and put the potato shells on it cut side down; bake until the cut sides are golden brown and the skin is crispy, about 20 minutes.

Pat the meat cubes dry with paper towels and season with salt and pepper. Heat 2 tablespoons olive oil in a large Dutch oven and sear the meat on all sides to a deep golden brown, about 10 minutes. Remove the meat to a plate and carefully add 1 tablespoon water to the hot pot, scraping up brown bits from bottom. Add 1 tablespoon olive oil and the pearl onions; season with salt and pepper. Cook about 7 minutes, stirring often, until the onions begin to caramelize, adding water as needed to deglaze brown bits from the bottom of the pot. When onions are deep golden brown, add the reduced beef stock and beef cubes and their juices to the pot and bring to a boil. Reduce the heat to maintain a simmer and cook until meat is tender, skimming fat off the top if necessary, 35 to 40 minutes.

Pass the reserved potato flesh through a ricer or mash with a masher until smooth, adding hot water to loosen. Add 1 tablespoon olive oil, season with salt and pepper, and mix well.

Ladle the stew into the crisp potato bowls, top with a spoon of mashed potatoes, and enjoy.

CLASSIC ROASTED LEG of LAMB

Whisk the salt, pepper, garlic, lemon juice and zest, mint, and olive oil together in a small bowl. Cover the lamb meat on all sides with the mixture and marinate in the refrigerator at least 8 hours or overnight.

Preheat the oven to 450°F and position rack to lower third of oven.

Let the marinated lamb sit out for 45 minutes before cooking. Place the lamb on a roasting rack in a roasting pan and pour 2 cups water into the bottom of the pan. Cover the bone with aluminum foil to prevent it from burning and transfer the lamb to the oven. Immediately lower the temperature to 350°F and cook until a thermometer reads 135°F at the thickest part of the leg, about 2 hours. Remove the lamb from the oven and tent with aluminum foil, allowing it to rest 15 to 20 minutes before carving.

Note: *To make carving easier, have your butcher cut the tendons that hold the meat to the bone, which allows the meat to pull away from the bone while roasting.*

2 teaspoons kosher salt

1 teaspoon freshly ground black pepper

4 garlic cloves, minced

Zest and juice of 2 lemons

1 large mint bunch, roughly chopped

⅓ cup olive oil

One 5- to 8-pound bone-in leg of lamb, silver skin removed

YIELD: 8 SERVINGS

What makes this recipe really sing:

When it's time to celebrate spring, I immediately think of this roasted lamb to go with all the incredible vegetables on their way to the farmer's market. The whole leg contains both marbled and leaner cuts of meat. This makes fantastic leftovers with a ton of uses! It's a great base for a quick shepherd's pie and a great stuffing for meat pies. My personal favorite is to stuff some into a pita and top it with a bit of Greek yogurt whipped with fresh chopped mint, a squeeze of lemon, and a pinch of cumin or turmeric.

What to toss in if you have it:

For a fantastic quick sauce, skim off the excess fat from the cooking liquid in the bottom of the roasting pan and put the pan on the stovetop; if necessary transfer it to a stovetop-safe pan. Over medium heat, add ½ cup white wine; bring the liquid to a boil; reduce to a simmer. Simmer until less than 1 cup of liquid remains and stir in a pat of cold butter and ½ cup of chopped fresh mint leaves. Serve with the lamb and enjoy!

DUCK BREASTS with CITRUS-PORT CHERRY SAUCE

Preheat the oven to 400°F.

With a knife, score the skin of the duck breasts in two directions, crossing over each other (making a crosshatch). Season both sides of each duck breast with salt and pepper.

In a large nonstick skillet, over medium-high heat, place the duck breasts skin side down. Sear until the skin is golden brown, about 10 minutes, flip, and sear the other side for just 3 minutes. Place seared duck breasts in a baking dish skin side up and put in the oven. Bake 12 minutes.

Meanwhile, pour off the excess fat from skillet and place the skillet back on the stovetop over medium heat. Add the shallots and sauté until translucent, 3 to 4 minutes. Add the port wine and orange juice and scrape up any brown bits on the bottom of the skillet; stir in the orange zest and chopped cherries and bring to a boil. Simmer for about 5 minutes to reduce and thicken the mixture, mashing the cherries with the back of a wooden spoon to extract flavor as they are cooking.

Remove the duck breasts from the oven and let them stand 5 minutes. Slice them into ¼-inch slices on a diagonal. Pour the citrus-port cherry sauce over the sliced duck breasts and enjoy!

Note: *Leftover duck fat is great for cooking potatoes or eggs.*

4 skin-on, boneless duck breasts

Kosher salt and freshly ground black pepper, to taste

1 large or 2 small shallots, minced

¼ cup ruby port wine

⅓ cup freshly squeezed orange juice plus 1 teaspoon orange zest

1 cup frozen pitted black cherries, thawed and roughly chopped

YIELD: 4 SERVINGS

What makes this recipe really sing:
Sweet sauces or compotes are a great match for darker meats such as duck or lamb. The tart-flavored dark cherries and port stand up well to the crispy skin and rich duck meat.

❧

What to toss in if you have it:
A splash of balsamic vinegar in the sauce will give it an acidic roundness and a few chopped chives will add color and a bit of fresh onion bite.

❧

BEER SHRIMP BOIL

Three 12-ounce bottles lager beer

1 cup water

1 tablespoon shrimp boil or
Creole seasoning

1 teaspoon kosher salt

1 teaspoon black peppercorns

Juice of 1 lemon, lemon
halves reserved

1/4 pound (1 stick) unsalted butter

1 1/2 pounds large shrimp, heads
on and in shell, rinsed well

YIELD: 4 SERVINGS

What makes this recipe really sing:

This is a southern happy hour on a plate.
The dark, creamy lager adds richness
to the shrimp and complements their
saltiness. Add some butter and roll up
your sleeves!

What to toss in if you have it:

Throw in some 1-inch pieces of corn on
the cob and some fresh crayfish for a real
traditional shrimp boil, and a quartered
jalapeño if you like it to bite you back.
(I love a great loaf of French bread with
this to sop up the yummy sauce!)

In a large pot, bring the beer, water, shrimp boil seasoning, salt, peppercorns, and the juiced lemon halves to a boil. Allow the mixture to boil, covered, 10 minutes. In the meantime, melt the butter in a small saucepan and add the lemon juice. Add the shrimp to the pot of boiling beer, cover, and turn off the heat. Check the shrimp after 3 minutes for pink color throughout; with a slotted spoon, remove the shrimp and transfer them to serving bowls.

Add 1/2 cup of the boiling beer liquid to the butter and simmer 2 minutes.

Serve the warm shrimp with the butter dipping sauce on the side and don't forget empty bowls for the shrimp shells. Enjoy!

CLASSIC SOUTHERN BLACKENED CATFISH

COMPOUND BUTTER:

¼ pound (1 stick) unsalted butter, at room temperature

1 tablespoon Creole seasoning (I use Tony Cachere's.)

Zest and juice of 1 lemon

¼ teaspoon kosher salt

⅛ teaspoon freshly cracked black pepper

1 tablespoon chopped chives

CATFISH:

2 lemons, thinly sliced

Compound Butter (recipe above), divided

Four 8-ounce fresh skinless, boneless catfish filets

¼ cup Creole seasoning

Whole chives, for garnish

YIELD: 4 SERVINGS

What makes this recipe really sing:
The combination of tart lemon and the rich compound butter is great with full-flavored catfish. Blackening the spiced filets in cast iron toasts the spices and releases the oils to flavor the fish—don't be tempted to skip this step or the dish has a completely different flavor.

What to toss in if you have it:
A splash of white wine or even beer in the baking dish with the lemons will add depth to the pan sauce. Simple white rice served alongside is great for soaking up the juices.

For the compound butter: In a bowl, mix the butter with the Creole seasoning, lemon zest and juice, salt, and pepper; mix in chopped chives and set aside. The butter can be made ahead and chilled; bring to room temperature before using.

For the catfish: Preheat the oven to 350°F.

Preheat a large well-seasoned cast-iron or nonstick skillet over medium-high heat.

Line the bottom of a 9 × 11-inch baking dish with the lemon slices and dollop half of the compound butter evenly over them. Evenly coat both sides of each fish filet with 1 tablespoon Creole seasoning. Working in batches, add the seasoned filets to the hot skillet and cook 2 minutes on each side to just toast and brown the seasoning. With a spatula, carefully place the seared fish on top of the buttered lemon slices in the baking dish. Bake until the fish easily break apart with a fork, 12 to 15 minutes. Immediately top each hot fillet with a spoonful of remaining compound butter; transfer to heated serving plates and garnish each filet with a few whole fresh chives.

SAKE and LEMONGRASS STEAMED SEA BASS

Preheat the oven to 425°F.

Prepare the lemongrass by removing the outer tough leaves to reveal the bulb's white center, retaining just the lower 3 inches of each stalk. Smash each bulb with the back of a knife to release the oils and flavor.

Lay the lime slices in the bottom of a baking dish. Evenly space the lemongrass pieces on top of the lime slices and lay the ginger slices evenly around the lemongrass. Place the filets directly on top of the lemongrass and ginger, pour the sake over the fish, and season with salt. Cover the dish with aluminum foil and bake until the fish is firm, opaque in the center, and beginning to flake, about 15 minutes. The cooking time will vary depending on the thickness of the filets.

Just before serving, spoon a little of the liquid from the baking dish over the filets and transfer them to plates.

4 lemongrass stalks

3 limes, sliced into thin rounds

One 2-inch piece fresh ginger, peeled and cut into thin coins

Four 6-ounce fresh skinless, boneless sea bass filets, preferably Chilean

1/3 cup sake, preferably unfiltered

Kosher salt, to taste

YIELD: 4 SERVINGS

What makes this recipe really sing:
You'll be surprised at how much flavor—especially pungent flavors like ginger and lime—a fresh piece of fish will take on when being steamed by this method. The sake adds a warm roundness; be sure to spoon some of the hot liquid over the fish just before serving.

What to toss in if you have it:
Toss a few sprigs of cilantro into the baking dish under the fish. Sea bass is an oily, rich fish and can stand up to ingredients with big flavors. Serve this fish with some steamed spinach and brown rice and your guests will think they are dining in a fine Japanese restaurant.

WHOLE STRIPED BASS BAKED in SALT

One 3-pound whole striped bass, gutted, cleaned, and scaled

4 cups kosher salt plus more to taste

Freshly cracked black pepper, to taste

2 lemons, thinly sliced and seeds removed plus 4 lemon wedges for garnish

½ fennel bulb, cored and thinly sliced, fronds removed for garnish

2 scallions, sliced

1 tablespoon fennel seeds

3 to 4 tablespoons water

YIELD: 4 SERVINGS

What makes this recipe really sing:
Baking fish in salt produces incredibly tender, moist meat. Be sure to pack the salt on just before you are ready to bake it, because if it sits too long, it will actually begin to draw the moisture from the meat and the curing process will begin. The fennel seeds in the salt crust impart a lovely anise aroma to the fish.

What to toss in if you have it:
Stuff some halved, pitted kalamata olives and a few slices of orange into the cavity of the fish for a sweet and salty Mediterranean twist.

Preheat the oven to 450°F.

Line a baking sheet with a silicone mat or parchment paper.

Rinse the fish and pat dry inside and out with a paper towel. Season the cavity well with salt and pepper and stuff the lemon slices, fennel, and scallions into the fish, enclosing inside the cavity completely.

In a bowl, mix the salt and fennel seeds together with 3 to 4 tablespoons water to moisten. Pour a third of the salt mixture onto the lined baking sheet and spread to roughly the size of the fish. Lay the stuffed fish on the salt mix and pour the remaining salt mix over the top. Use your hands to evenly spread it to completely enclose the fish and press lightly.

Bake in the oven for 40 minutes. Remove the fish and let stand 10 minutes before carefully cracking the outer salt crust, exposing the whole fish. Carefully remove the skin and lift the fish filet off the bones, transferring it to a serving platter. Pull the skeleton from the fish by lifting the tail and discard. Remove the remaining filet meat to the platter.

Garnish the fish with lemon wedges and sprinkle fennel fronds over the top. Serve immediately.

The fish in the process of ultimately being enclosed by the salt.

CLAIRE'S CARBONARA

Salt for the pot

½ pound slab bacon, cut into
½-inch chunks

1 pound fresh or dried
spinach fettuccine

1 large egg plus 2 large egg yolks,
at room temperature

1 cup grated Parmigiano-Reggiano
cheese plus more for garnish

2 teaspoons freshly cracked
black pepper, or to taste

2 cups baby spinach leaves,
well rinsed

YIELD: 4 SERVINGS

What makes this recipe really sing:
Bacon and eggs on pasta? It seriously
doesn't get better than this in the
comfort food category. The spinach
leaves add a fresh vegetable bite.

What to toss in if you have it:
Add some fresh peas and lemon zest into
the pasta while you toss it with the eggs
and cheese for a light "springy" twist.

Bring a large pot of water to a boil and salt generously.

Put the bacon in a large high-sided skillet and cook over medium-high heat until crisp, about 10 minutes. Remove the skillet from the heat.

When the bacon is about halfway cooked, drop the pasta into the boiling water and cook about 4 minutes for fresh, or according to the package instructions if using dried. Remove about 1 cup of pasta water and drain the pasta.

Meanwhile, whisk the egg and egg yolks, 1 cup Parmigiano-Reggiano cheese, and pepper together in a small bowl.

Return the bacon-drippings skillet to medium heat and carefully pour in ½ cup of pasta cooking water. When it's very hot, remove it from the heat and add the hot pasta, tossing with tongs to coat. While tossing continually, slowly drizzle the egg mixture over the pasta until it is completely coated. If the pasta is not still steaming hot, return the skillet to low heat while tossing. Add more cooking water if the pasta seems dry. Toss the pasta with the spinach leaves until evenly distributed. Serve immediately with more cheese sprinkled over the top.

Note: *The key to perfect carbonara is working while everything is piping hot; this assures the egg will cook and produce a silky, creamy sauce that sticks to the pasta.*

SUNDAY POT ROAST
with MUSHROOM GRAVY

One 4- to 5-pound boneless beef
bottom round roast

Kosher salt and freshly cracked
black pepper, to taste

2 tablespoons olive oil

1 pound cremini mushrooms,
cleaned and quartered

2 medium yellow onions,
halved and sliced

4 cups low-sodium
beef broth

YIELD: 4 SERVINGS WITH
LEFTOVERS!

What makes this recipe really sing:
There's nothing more comforting
than the smell of pot roast in the
oven. Take the time to really brown
the meat and mushrooms before
slipping the pot into the oven—
a technique that makes a world of
difference in its depth of flavor. This
meat makes an incredible sandwich
the next day! I love to use it for
sourdough bread paninis with a smoky
Gouda cheese. It also makes
the ultimate base for shepherd's pie,
and I use it as a quick add for
stew as well!

What to toss in if you have it:
Pour a cup of dry red wine into the
pot once the mushrooms are brown
to make a deep red-wine gravy; a
couple of garlic cloves and a sprig of
thyme will add more flavor as well.

Preheat the oven to 325°F.

Pat the meat dry with paper towels and season well on all sides with salt
and pepper. Heat the oil in a large Dutch oven over medium-high heat,
add the roast and brown all sides, about 4 minutes per side. Transfer the
roast to a plate and add the mushrooms to the pot; season with salt and
pepper and cook, stirring occasionally, until browned and beginning to
release liquid, about 5 minutes.

Add the onions and broth and stir until combined. Nestle the roast into
the vegetables, adding any juices it released to the pot. Add the beef broth,
bring to a simmer, cover, and transfer to the oven and roast 2½ hours.
Remove the lid, carefully flip the roast, and continue cooking 30 minutes;
the roast should be fork-tender and liquid reduced.

Remove the pot from the oven, transfer the roast to a cutting board and
tent with foil to keep warm; let the mushrooms and onions stand several
minutes undisturbed to allow some of the beef fat to rise to the surface.
With a large spoon, skim the excess fat and discard. With a ladle, add about
1½ cups mushrooms and onions with some cooking liquid to the jar of
a blender or bowl of a food processor. Carefully puree the mixture until
very smooth. Pour the puree back into the pot and stir very well until
combined; taste and adjust seasoning.

To serve, slice the pot roast and arrange on a serving platter. Drizzle some
mushroom gravy over the top and pass the extra gravy at the table.

EASY WHITE PIZZA

Preheat the oven to 400°F. Adjust the oven rack to the lower third of the oven.

Brush the pizza pan with oil. With your hands, on a work surface, press the pizza dough into a large flat disk and transfer to the greased pan. Using your fingers, press the dough onto the pan until it has stretched to the perimeter of the pan. Create a dough "lip" around the outer edges of the pan. Brush the entire surface of the dough lightly with garlic oil and pierce the bottom of the dough all over with a fork to prevent bubbling.

Evenly spread the mozzarella over the dough. With two spoons, dollop teaspoon-size mounds of ricotta evenly over the mozzarella. Season the top of the pizza with salt and pepper and evenly sprinkle the oregano leaves over all.

Bake in the lower third of the oven until the crust is golden brown and the cheese is bubbly and browning on top, 25 to 30 minutes. Cool on the pan for 10 minutes before garnishing with additional oregano and slicing into eight pieces.

Note: *Try buying fresh pizza dough from your local pizzeria; just be sure to let it sit out at room temperature for a few minutes, as warmer dough is easier to work with.*

Garlic-flavored olive oil

1 pound ball frozen pizza dough, thawed and at room temperature

3 cups shredded mozzarella cheese

1/2 cup whole milk ricotta cheese

Kosher salt and freshly cracked black pepper, to taste

2 teaspoons chopped fresh oregano leaves plus more for garnish

SPECIAL EQUIPMENT:
14-inch-round pizza pan

YIELD: 4 SERVINGS

What makes this recipe really sing:
Pizza at home just doesn't get any easier than this—no sauce required! The garlic oil on the crust helps crisp and flavor it; the combination of fresh oregano, ricotta, and mozzarella is classic—you'll think you stepped into a New York pizzeria for a late-night slice!

What to toss in if you have it:
Finely chop some broccoli florets and scatter them over the pizza before baking. If you like a meat pizza, browned sweet fennel sausage or diced chicken go great with this cheese combination.

FIG and BLUE CHEESE TART

1 sheet frozen puff pastry, thawed in refrigerator

2 tablespoons extra-virgin olive oil

2 large Vidalia or other sweet onions, thinly sliced

6 large dried Calimyrna or green figs, chopped

Kosher salt and freshly cracked black pepper, to taste

½ cup water

2 ounces blue cheese, such as Maytag, crumbled

YIELD: 4 TO 6 SERVINGS

What makes this recipe really sing:

A fantastic main dish for vegetarians! I also love to make this tart to change up side dishes; it tastes great with steak or roasted meats. The super sweet Vidalias get even sweeter when caramelized, and the blue cheese adds a sharp saltiness to this rich but easy recipe.

What to toss in if you have it:

Add a couple of sprigs of fresh thyme to the onions while they cook, then pull out the stems before you assemble the tart. Thyme and onions are a natural match, and the herb will add earthiness to the tart.

Preheat the oven to 400°F.

Line a baking sheet with parchment paper.

On a work surface, roll the puff pastry into a roughly 10 × 16-inch rectangle and transfer it to the baking sheet. With a sharp knife, trim the uneven edges to make a perfect rectangle. Using a ruler as a guide, score a 1-inch border around the outer edge of the dough with the knife without cutting completely through. With a fork, pierce the interior of the tart shell all over to prevent rising; do not pierce the scored border. Bake about 15 minutes, or until the outer edges have puffed and are golden in color; set aside.

Heat 2 tablespoons olive oil in a large skillet over medium-low heat. Add the onions and figs and season well with salt and pepper. Cook, stirring occasionally, until the onions begin to brown; add water, a tablespoon at a time, as the skillet gets dry, scraping and stirring the brown bits that are stuck to the skillet. When the onions are caramelized to a dark golden color, remove from the heat.

When ready to serve, preheat the oven to 350°F. Evenly spread the caramelized onions and figs on the cooked pastry shell; top with the blue cheese crumbles and heat in the oven until warmed through, 5 to 7 minutes. Remove from oven, cut into wedges, serve warm or at room temperature.

6.

SIDEKICKS

VEGETABLE DISHES TO DRESS UP ANY PLATE

Probably the best way to utilize five-ingredient cooking is in the side dish department. This is the place to really experiment and have fun. Sometimes the most unlikely combinations can become all-stars in your recipe file, like cauliflower with dates or green beans with blue cheese. These side dishes are so good, you may opt to drop the entrée altogether!

BRUSSELS SPROUTS GRATIN

Preheat the oven to 400°F.

Bring a large pot of salted water to a boil. Add the Brussels sprouts and cook 5 to 7 minutes, until bright green and beginning to soften; drop into a bowl of ice water to stop the cooking process.

Make the sauce by melting the butter and flour together in a saucepan over medium heat. Cook, stirring, until smooth and bubbling, about 1 minute; slowly whisk in the milk and continue to cook, whisking frequently, until thick and creamy, 2 to 3 minutes. Add ¼ of the cheese and stir until melted and smooth. Season the sauce well with salt and heavily with pepper.

Halve the Brussels sprouts through the core and put them in an even layer in a 2-quart baking dish. Pour the sauce over the sprouts and evenly top with the remaining cheese. Bake in the center of the oven 10 to 15 minutes, until golden and bubbling on top.

2 pints Brussels sprouts, (about 1 ½ pounds), trimmed

3 tablespoons unsalted butter

3 tablespoons unbleached all-purpose flour

2 cups milk, at room temperature

5 ounces Gruyère cheese, grated (about 1 cup grated)

Kosher salt and freshly cracked black pepper, to taste

YIELD: 6 TO 8 SERVINGS

What makes this recipe really sing:
Even the hardiest Brussels sprouts-haters will like this dish—they're covered in cheese sauce! Nutty, buttery Gruyère is a perfect companion for them and this dish is a great side for chicken, pork, or roasted meats.

What to toss in if you have it:
Whisk a teaspoon or two of dry mustard and a pinch of grated nutmeg into the milk to add a bit of warm spice and richness to the sauce. Some toasted chopped hazelnuts sprinkled over the top just before serving will add some crunch.

INDIAN CORN
with CURRY YOGURT

Preheat a stovetop grill pan to medium-high heat. Grill the corn, turning frequently, until evenly browned, 10 to 12 minutes.

In a small bowl, stir together the yogurt, honey, lime juice, and curry until smooth.

Transfer the corn to a cutting board, cut the cobs in half crosswise, and serve immediately with a drizzle of curry yogurt, a sprinkling of salt and pepper, and a squeeze of a lime wedge. The corn can also be refrigerated and served cold.

4 fresh large sweet corn cobs, husks and silk removed

One 7-ounce container Greek yogurt

1 tablespoon honey

Juice of 1 lime plus 4 lime wedges for serving

1 teaspoon curry powder

Kosher salt and freshly cracked black pepper, to taste

YIELD: 4 SERVINGS

What makes this recipe really sing:
I am crazy about that Mexican-style grilled corn with mayonnaise, Cotija cheese, and chili powder, so I thought I'd put an Indian spin on it. The results are fantastic; the tart but sweet curry yogurt drizzled over the grilled corn is really unexpected and lip smacking!

What to toss in if you have it:
To round out the curry Indian flavor, toss some chopped fresh cilantro and a little cayenne pepper over the corn after you slather it with the yogurt sauce. What a perfect "fusion" of cultures—the American picnic and Indian curry bar.

NUTTY GREEN BEANS with BLUE CHEESE and BACON

Kosher salt, to taste

1 pound haricots verts (baby French green beans), trimmed

3 slices smoked bacon

4 ounces Shropshire blue cheese, or your favorite blue cheese, crumbled

1 1/2 cups toasted whole pecans, coarsely chopped

Freshly cracked black pepper, to taste

YIELD: 4 SERVINGS

What makes this recipe really sing:
This easy side dish is a real showstopper—good enough for company or a holiday table. It combines some of my favorite ingredients, including Shropshire blue, an orange-tinged aged blue cheese with the nutty flavor of Stilton but still meltable. Look for it in your cheese shop or specialty market—it is great alone for dessert, drizzled with honey, and with a glass of port.

ॐ

What to toss in if you have it:
The earthy flavor of pecans is perfect with the beans but if you have pistachios, walnuts, or sliced almonds, they will add a nice crunch as well. You can also purchase candied nuts for salads—try some with the green beans for even more sweet and spicy punch.

ॐ

Bring a large pot of salted water to a boil over high heat. Add the haricots verts and cook for about 2 minutes. With a slotted spoon or strainer, transfer the beans to a large bowl of ice water to stop the cooking. Once they're cooled, drain the beans and reserve.

In a large skillet over medium heat, cook the bacon until crisp; transfer to a paper towel–lined plate to drain. Add the beans to the bacon drippings and cook over medium heat 2 to 3 minutes. Add the blue cheese and toss just until it starts to melt. Break the cooked bacon into bite-size pieces and add to the skillet. Finish by stirring in the toasted chopped pecans; season with the freshly cracked black pepper and just a tiny pinch of kosher salt. Serve immediately.

ROASTED CAULIFLOWER
with DATES and PINE NUTS

Preheat the oven to 425°F.

Evenly spread the cauliflower on a baking sheet and season with salt and pepper. Transfer to the oven and roast, tossing once with a spatula, until golden brown at the edges, about 20 minutes.

Put the butter in a small skillet over medium-low heat. Once it's melted, add the pine nuts and cook, stirring frequently, until they're light golden brown, about 5 minutes. Add the garlic and dates and continue cooking until the garlic and dates are softened, 2 to 3 minutes more; season with salt.

Transfer the hot cauliflower to a serving bowl, drizzle the pine nut mixture over the top, and toss to combine. Taste and adjust seasoning if necessary and serve warm or at room temperature.

1 large head cauliflower, cut into florets (about 8 cups)

Kosher salt and freshly cracked black pepper, to taste

4 tablespoons unsalted butter

⅓ cup pine nuts

1 garlic clove, minced

½ cup pitted Medjool dates, coarsely chopped

YIELD: 4 TO 6 SERVINGS

What makes this recipe really sing:
This may seem like a strange combination, but many types of cuisines combine sweet elements, such as dried fruit, with vegetables. Add the crunch of pine nuts, the golden brown cauliflower, and the nutty flavor of the browned butter, and this will be a new favorite in your side dish recipe file.

What to toss in if you have it:
Sprinkle the zest of half a lemon over the warm cauliflower before serving for a tart edge. Or, to really "Italianize" the dish, toss half a teaspoon of chopped fresh rosemary into the butter and pine nuts before tossing with the cauliflower.

CLASSIC COLESLAW

1 head green cabbage, cored and finely sliced

2 large carrots, peeled and grated

8 ounces crème fraîche

3 tablespoons honey

1/3 cup cider vinegar

Kosher salt and freshly cracked black pepper, to taste

YIELD: 6 SERVINGS

What makes this recipe really sing:
I love the tangy flavors of crème fraîche and yogurt and use them a lot in place of mayonnaise. I use crème fraîche in coleslaw dressing because it adds more tang; combined with the honey and cider vinegar, which is a little sweeter than plain white vinegar, makes a dressing that's bottle-worthy.

What to toss in if you have it:
Coleslaw is like a blank canvas; you can add herbs, spices, nuts, vegetables, and even dried fruit to make it your own. This version is particularly good with a pinch of celery seed and some thinly sliced scallions thrown into the mix.

Toss the cabbage and carrots together in a mixing bowl to combine. In a small bowl, whisk the crème fraîche, honey, and vinegar together until smooth; season well with salt and pepper and pour over the cabbage mixture.

Toss the coleslaw until evenly coated with the dressing; taste and adjust the seasoning. Let stand at least 30 minutes before serving.

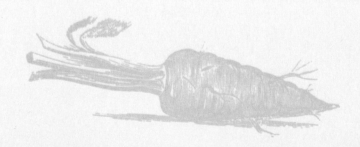

BRAISED RED CABBAGE

Heat a large Dutch oven over medium-high heat; add the bacon slices and cook until crisp, about 5 minutes. Transfer the bacon to a paper towel–lined plate to drain. Add the shallot to the pot and cook until just light golden, 3 to 4 minutes. Pour in the vinegar, scraping the pot to release any browned bits, and simmer 2 to 3 minutes. Add the cabbage, tossing to coat and soften slightly; pour in the stock and season with pepper and lightly with salt. Reduce heat to a simmer, cover, and cook, stirring occasionally, until cabbage is very soft, about 30 minutes.

Remove the lid and cook, stirring occasionally, 5 minutes more to allow the moisture to evaporate and cooking liquid to thicken. Transfer to a serving dish, top with crumbled bacon, and enjoy!

3 slices maple-flavored bacon

1 small shallot, peeled and sliced

1/3 cup balsamic vinegar

1/2 head red cabbage, cored and thinly sliced

1 cup chicken stock

Kosher salt and freshly cracked black pepper, to taste

YIELD: 4 SERVINGS

What makes this recipe really sing:
Cooked cabbage really gets a bad rap. Adding some maple-flavored bacon adds some smoky, salty sweetness, and the vinegar and chicken stock add tang and richness. Plus, it's virtually impossible to overcook cabbage—it has a great texture even after cooking it for a long time. This is so easy and so delicious… you have to try it!

What to toss in if you have it:
If you have some whole-grain Dijon, stir a spoonful into the braising liquid along with some golden raisins at the end. You'll enhance the tart vinegar flavor and the sweetness at the same time.

CRUNCHY STIR-FRIED SNOW PEAS with CASHEWS

2 tablespoons vegetable oil

1 pound snow peas, trimmed

3 tablespoons seasoned rice vinegar

1 tablespoon soy sauce

1/2 cup roasted salted cashews, coarsely chopped, plus whole ones for garnish

Freshly ground black pepper, to taste

YIELD: 4 SERVINGS

What makes this recipe really sing:
The trick to successful stir-frying is cooking quickly over high heat. Don't be afraid, just make sure to keep the vegetables moving so they don't burn or overcook. The snow peas should still have a crisp snap when you bite into them. The mix of rice vinegar and soy sauce creates a sweet and salty glaze.

What to toss in if you have it:
Chopped shallots are great in this dish—just throw them in with the snow peas and remember to keep moving the vegetables so they don't scorch. Some chopped baby corn would add a colorful, nutritious crunch with the cashews.

Heat the oil in a large nonstick skillet or wok over medium-high heat. Add the snow peas and cook, tossing them in the skillet or stirring constantly until bright green and the edges are beginning to brown, 4 to 5 minutes.

Mix the rice vinegar and soy sauce in a small bowl. Pour the liquid into the skillet and cook until some of the liquid evaporates, about 1 minute. Toss in the cashews and a few grinds of black pepper and stir the vegetables until evenly coated and hot.

Transfer to a serving platter, sprinkle whole cashews over the top, and serve immediately.

GINGERED BUTTERNUT SQUASH FLAMBÉ

Melt the butter in a large skillet over medium-low heat; add the minced ginger and cook, stirring frequently, until the ginger has mostly dissolved and sugar is melted, 6 to 8 minutes. Add the squash, and season with salt and pepper and toss to coat; cook, partially covered, stirring often, until the squash is cooked through but still holds its shape, about 15 minutes.

Increase the heat to medium high and add the lime juice. Stir until the squash has absorbed the juice and the skillet is very hot. Carefully pour in the rum and, if you're cooking on a gas stovetop, gently tilt the skillet to ignite the alcohol. If you have an electric stove, you can light it with a match or lighter. Cook, shaking the skillet, until the flame dies out and the alcohol has mostly evaporated.

Stir the squash well, taste, and adjust the seasoning if necessary. Serve warm.

---

4 tablespoons unsalted butter

2 tablespoons minced candied ginger

1 small butternut squash, peeled, seeded, and cut into 1/2-inch cubes

Kosher salt and freshly cracked black pepper, to taste

Juice of 1 lime

1/4 cup spiced dark rum, such as Captain Morgan

YIELD: 4 SERVINGS

What makes this recipe really sing:
Butternut squash is the unsung hero of the kitchen. There are literally hundreds of ways to prepare it, and since I love ginger, I thought it would taste great with squash, and I was right. Candied ginger adds the heat of fresh gingerroot along with some sweetness from the sugar.

What to toss in if you have it:
To add a savory element, stir in a heaping tablespoon of Dijon mustard before adding the rum; some toasted chopped pecans sprinkled over the top will make this side dish special enough for a holiday.

FRESH PEA RAVIOLI with CRISPY PROSCIUTTO

2 tablespoons lemon-infused olive oil plus more for serving

4 slices prosciutto, about ¼ cup cut into thin strips (julienned)

1 cup, 12 ounces fresh whole-milk ricotta

1 ½ cups fresh-shelled English peas

Kosher salt, to taste

Water

Freshly cracked pepper, to taste

1-package wonton wrappers, size is optional

YIELD: 4 TO 6 SERVINGS

What makes this recipe really sing:
This is an incredibly versatile recipe. Serve a small portion as a first course appetizer at a dinner party, or as a side dish for any meal, or even as a stand-alone entrée for lunch or dinner. When peas are fresh and so incredibly sweet, I find myself making this recipe again and again to rave reviews each time.

What to toss in if you have it:
I really love this one just as it is, but every once in a while I throw a fresh herb in the pea-ricotta filling. Fresh mint is my favorite, but basil, oregano, or even thyme are lovely as well. Just add 1 chopped teaspoon or more, to taste, of your favorite fresh herb in the filling mix and enjoy!

Heat oil in a skillet and add the prosciutto, stirring until crisp. Remove and drain on paper towels. Lightly oil a serving plate with prosciutto crisping oil and place in a warm oven until ready to serve.

Drain the ricotta of excess moisture in a fine mesh sieve for 7 to 10 minutes.

Bring a large pot of salted water to a boil. Blanche peas in water, just 2 to 3 minutes cook until just tender and transfer to an ice-cold water bath, shocking to stop cooking and preserve color. Keep pot of hot water to cook ravioli.

Reserve ¼ cup of blanched peas for garnish and transfer remaining 1 ¼ cups peas to a food processor and puree with drained ricotta, salt and pepper to taste. Place a teaspoon (or more depending on wonton size) of pea-ricotta mixture in the center of each wonton wrapper; avoid overfilling. Dampen the inside outer edges of wonton with water and fold, pinching around borders to ensure ravioli are well sealed.

In batches, to not overfill pot, drop ravioli into boiling water and cook until tender and the wrapper becomes slightly translucent, about 3 minutes. With a slotted spoon or skimmer, transfer cooked ravioli to the lightly oiled serving plate. Drizzle with lemon-infused olive oil and top with crispy prosciutto. Garnish with a few blanched peas.

SMOKY ROASTED PEACHES

Preheat the oven to 400°F.

Cut the onion and red bell pepper into rough chunks and put in a bowl; mince the jalapeños and add them. Drizzle 1 tablespoon of the extra-virgin olive oil over the vegetables and toss. Add a good pinch of salt and some pepper, toss, and place on one side of a rimmed baking sheet.

Drizzle the peaches with remaining tablespoon of oil, being sure to coat the cut sides well; put them cut side down on the other side of the baking sheet. Roast the fruit and vegetables for 25 minutes or until caramelized. Using tongs, pull the skin off the peach halves and discard.

Serve two peach halves per person cut side up on a bed of the roasted red bell peppers, onions, and jalapeños.

Note: *If freestone peaches are not available, split the peaches leaving the pits intact; they can be removed easily after roasting.*

1 red onion, skin removed

1 red bell pepper, stemmed, seeded, and ribs removed

2 jalapeños, stemmed, seeded, and ribs removed

2 tablespoons extra-virgin olive oil, divided

Kosher salt and freshly cracked black pepper

4 ripe fresh freestone peaches, halved and pitted

YIELD: 4 SERVINGS

What makes this recipe really sing:
There is something special about using fruits in unexpected ways. Roasting the peaches brings out all their sweet juices, and the kick from the jalapeño makes this a really great side for a barbecue. I love to chop the peaches and toss it all together to serve like a warm chutney, complimenting almost any grilled meal.

What to toss in if you have it:
A bit of chopped cilantro or parsley before serving is a nice pop of color and flavor.

EASY RATATOUILLE

2 tablespoons garlic-infused olive oil plus more as needed

1 medium red onion

1 large purple eggplant, cut into 1/2-inch cubes

Kosher salt and freshly ground black pepper, to taste

1 large tomato, seeded and finely diced

1 tablespoon small brined capers plus 1 tablespoon brine from the jar

---

YIELD: 4 SERVINGS

What makes this recipe really sing:
Ratatouille goes well with just about any meat. You can serve it with grilled lamb chops, steak, or even stuffed into flounder filets and baked. This version has a nice, savory, mild garlic flavor, with some tangy bite from the capers and brine.

What to toss in if you have it:
Soak some golden raisins or currants in hot water until they are plumped, then stir them in along with the tomatoes and capers to add a sweetness to each bite. Golden toasted pine nuts are also a classic ingredient and add a nice crunchy texture.

Heat the garlic oil in a large skillet over medium heat; add the onion and cook until softened, about 5 minutes. Add the eggplant, season with salt and pepper, and cook, stirring gently every few minutes until soft, about 10 minutes. Add the tomatoes, capers, and caper brine and continue cooking until very hot and the tomato is just beginning to break down, about 5 minutes more.

Taste and adjust the seasoning, drizzling a little more garlic oil over it if necessary; serve warm or at room temperature.

ROASTED ASPARAGUS with BALSAMIC BROWNED BUTTER

Preheat the oven to 425°F.

Spread the asparagus out in an even layer on a baking sheet. Drizzle the olive oil over it, season with salt and pepper, and toss until coated. Transfer to the oven and roast, shaking the baking sheet occasionally to toss the asparagus, until they are beginning to brown and the tips are getting crisp, 12 to 15 minutes.

Meanwhile, melt the butter in a small skillet over medium-low heat; let the butter bubble and simmer until the milk solids just begin to turn light golden, about 5 minutes. Carefully add the vinegar and swirl the skillet over the heat until very hot, about 1 minute more.

Transfer the asparagus to a shallow serving platter, swirl the balsamic butter in the skillet, and pour it evenly over the asparagus. Sprinkle the cheese over the top and serve immediately.

1 ½ pounds medium asparagus, trimmed

2 tablespoons extra-virgin olive oil

Kosher salt and freshly cracked black pepper, to taste

3 tablespoons unsalted butter

1 tablespoon aged balsamic vinegar

2 ounces aged ricotta salata, crumbled

YIELD: 4 SERVINGS

What makes this recipe really sing:
I love browned butter on just about anything! Add the sweet and tart flavor of aged balsamic and you have an instant restaurant-worthy sauce. Roasting the asparagus at very high heat will keep it crisp and not mushy. The slightly salty, firm, ricotta salata pairs with the sweet vinegar perfectly.

What to toss in if you have it:
Add some drained capers to the butter sauce for a briny bite. If you can't find ricotta salata, use a vegetable peeler to shave some good Parmigiano-Reggiano or Pecorino Romano shavings over the warm asparagus.

GRANDMA MOORE'S CREAMED CORN

6 slices bacon

8 fresh large sweet corn cobs, preferably white, husks and silk removed

Kosher salt and freshly cracked black pepper, to taste

YIELD: 4 SERVINGS

What makes this recipe really sing:
There simply isn't anything more delicious than freshly picked sweet corn in the height of summer. Its starchy liquid is what thickens and "creams" the corn soup with no additions of cream or butter. Don't be tempted to shuck corn at the farmer's market or supermarket; leave the husk on until you're just ready to cook—it will help keep the moisture and sweetness at their peak.

What to toss in if you have it:
Absolutely nothing. Grandma Moore got it right—don't mess with perfection. Creamed corn is among the simplest expression of great food at its core: quality seasonal ingredients plus the right technique produce a winner every time.

In a large skillet (seasoned cast-iron does well here), cook the bacon over medium-high heat until crisp; transfer to a paper towel–lined plate, remove skillet from the heat, and reserve the drippings.

On a cutting board, cut the stalk ends of the corn cobs to make a flat surface; stand them up and shave the corn from the cobs with a sharp chef's knife. Return the skillet to medium-low heat and add the corn kernels. With the back of the knife, firmly scrape the cobs over a shallow plate to extract as much liquid (milk) as possible; add it to the skillet.

Season the corn lightly with salt and pepper and cook until broken down and creamy, 30 to 45 minutes, stirring often; add water if skillet gets too dry. Serve warm or at room temperature.

Note: *Crisp bacon can be crumbled over the creamed corn for garnish or reserved for another use. If you have bacon drippings on hand, use ½ cup for this recipe.*

SMOKY COLLARD GREENS

3 tablespoons olive oil

1 medium yellow onion, sliced

1 teaspoon sweet smoked paprika

¼ teaspoon cayenne pepper

Kosher salt and freshly cracked black pepper, to taste

2 ½ pounds collard or mustard greens (about 2 large bunches), washed and woody stems removed

---

YIELD: 4 SERVINGS

What makes this recipe really sing:
The classic preparation of collard greens usually has a smoked turkey wing or ham hock in it. My version is much lighter and quicker to prepare and has every bit as much flavor from the smoked paprika and hint of heat from the cayenne.

What to toss in if you have it:
If you like collard greens with a real punch, add a splash of cider vinegar to the pot while it cooks down. A couple of smashed whole garlic cloves will also deepen the flavor.

Heat the olive oil in a large Dutch oven over medium-high heat. Add the onion, paprika, and cayenne, season with salt and pepper, and cook, stirring occasionally, until the onion is softened, about 5 minutes. Add ½ cup water to the pot; once the water is simmering, add the greens (you may have to pack them in). Season generously with salt and pepper and cover with a lid; cook for 10 minutes. Remove the lid, toss the greens well with tongs, reduce the heat to medium low, and continue simmering until the greens are completely cooked and nearly all the liquid has evaporated, about 10 minutes more. Taste and adjust seasoning; serve warm.

TOMATO and VIDALIA ONION GRATIN

Preheat the oven to 350°F.

Render the bacon in a large skillet over medium heat. Remove the cooked bacon along with 2 tablespoons of the bacon fat; pour the fat over the bread crumbs and toss to coat. Add the onion rounds to the skillet in batches and cook, without breaking the round slices apart, until there is some golden color, 5 to 6 minutes per side.

To assemble the gratin, overlap the tomato slices in one row in a large baking dish, about 9 × 11 inches. Next, make a row, slightly overlapping, of the partially cooked onion rounds, being careful to keep the slices intact. Repeat until all tomatoes and onions are used; season the tomatoes and onions heavily with pepper and lightly with salt. Crumble the bacon over the vegetables; sprinkle the grated cheddar over the top followed by the bread crumbs. Bake 30 to 45 minutes, or until the cheese is bubbly; if the top is getting too brown, loosely cover with foil. Serve immediately.

1/4 pound bacon

1 cup fresh bread crumbs

2 large Vidalia onions, peeled and sliced into 1/4-inch-thick rounds

4 large heirloom or beefsteak tomatoes, sliced 1/4-inch thick

Kosher salt and freshly cracked black pepper

6 ounces sharp white cheddar cheese, grated (about 1 1/2 cups)

YIELD: 4 TO 6 SERVINGS

What makes this recipe really sing:
I originally made this gratin with green tomatoes as an alternative to fried, but thought the deep flavor of a ripe summer heirloom would be fantastic as well. I was right! Visit the farmer's market in July and August and support your local growers. You really can't go wrong with this dish—roasting them with onions and cheese enhances not-so-ripe tomatoes, and really showcases the perfectly ripe as well.

What to toss in if you have it:
Lightly dust some sliced shallots in seasoned flour and shallow fry them in olive oil until crisp. Sprinkle them over the gratin before serving it for additional crunch and sweet onion flavor.

SAUTÉED WILD MUSHROOMS

¼ cup olive oil plus more
as needed

2 pounds mixed wild
mushrooms, sliced

3 sprigs fresh thyme

Kosher salt and freshly ground
black pepper, to taste

2 shallots, chopped

¼ cup water

2 tablespoons
Worcestershire sauce

YIELD: 4 TO 6 SERVINGS

What makes this recipe really sing:
Mushrooms are so meaty and
flavorful, they don't need much to
coax out their best flavor, just correct
cooking technique. The key is to
not crowd the pan so that the
mushrooms brown. They give off
a lot of moisture, so if there are too
many in the pan, they will just steam
instead of develop the deep intense
flavor when they are golden brown.

What to toss in if you have it:
To make this really decadent, add
about ½ cup heavy cream at the
end of cooking and simmer it until
very thick and creamy; stir in about
2 tablespoons of sour cream for
a rich stroganoff-style mushroom
side dish.

Working in batches, pour 1 to 2 tablespoons olive oil in a large skillet over medium-high heat. Add about a third of the mushrooms and a sprig of thyme, depending on the skillet size, and cook, stirring, until golden brown and softened, about 10 minutes. Season the mushrooms with salt and pepper and transfer to a bowl. Cover to keep warm while you continue cooking the mushrooms with the thyme.

Once all the mushrooms are cooked, return them to the skillet and add the shallots. Stir and continue cooking until the shallots are softened, about 5 minutes. Pour about ¼ cup water and the Worcestershire sauce into the skillet and scrape up any brown bits. Continue cooking until the liquid is absorbed; taste and adjust seasoning. Serve warm or at room temperature.

CREAMY ROASTED BROCCOLI

2 pounds fresh broccoli (about 2 large bunches), florets removed, divided

¼ cup olive oil

Juice of 1 large orange plus 2 teaspoons orange zest

Coarse salt and freshly cracked black pepper, to taste

1 ½ cups heavy cream

2 large garlic cloves, peeled and smashed

YIELD: 6 TO 8 SERVINGS

What makes this recipe really sing:
This yummy comfort food is part soup, part side dish; the combination of pureed broccoli and roasted crisp florets is a new way of enjoying this vegetable. Although the combination of orange and broccoli may sound odd, just think of your favorite Chinese food combinations with orange and you'll understand why I love this dish so much.

What to toss in if you have it:
Chop some sweet Vidalia onion and add it to the broccoli and cream for fuller vegetable flavor. If you have some salted cashews in the house, coarsely chop them and sprinkle them over the top just before serving.

Preheat the oven to 425°F.

Put ⅔ of the broccoli in a large bowl with the olive oil and orange juice; season with salt and pepper and toss well to coat. Transfer the broccoli to a large rimmed baking sheet, arrange in one layer, and roast for approximately 15 minutes until just tender with golden brown edges.

Meanwhile, pour the cream into a medium heavy-bottomed saucepan, add the remaining broccoli, garlic, and orange zest and bring to a gentle simmer over medium-low heat. Cook until the cream is reduced to half its original volume and broccoli is cooked through, about 10 minutes.

With a handheld immersion blender or potato masher, or in a food processor, blend or pulse the cream and broccoli mixture until coarsely blended and still a bit chunky. Gently fold in the roasted broccoli until combined; taste and adjust seasoning if necessary. Transfer to a serving bowl and serve warm.

CARROT and TOASTED CUMIN SEED SALAD

Grate the carrots on the large holes of a box grater and put them in a bowl. Put the cumin seeds in a small skillet and toast over medium heat, shaking the skillet frequently until the cumin is fragrant, about 3 minutes. Add the cumin seeds, lemon zest and juice, olive oil and chopped cilantro to the carrots and toss. Season well with salt and pepper and toss until well combined.

Serve immediately at room temperature or refrigerate until ready to serve.

2 large carrots, peeled

1 teaspoon cumin seeds

Zest of 1 lemon plus juice of ½ lemon

2 tablespoons extra-virgin olive oil

¼ cup coarsely chopped fresh cilantro or mint leaves

Kosher salt and freshly cracked black pepper, to taste

YIELD: 4 SERVINGS

What makes this recipe really sing:
This tasty little side dish reminds me of all those little relishes you get in Vietnamese and Thai restaurants. The key to pulling the most flavor out of dried spices is to toast them; your whole house will smell wonderful when you warm the cumin seeds and toss them with the carrots and zippy lemon zest. This dish takes only minutes to make but tastes much more complicated.

What to toss in if you have it:
Sambal oelek, a vinegar-based condiment made from ground chili peppers, is fantastic with the grated carrot if you like some spice. Sliced scallions are also terrific to add a fresh green-onion flavor.

ROASTED SPAGHETTI SQUASH with BASIL BUTTER

Preheat the oven to 375°F.

Halve the squash through the stem and remove the seeds. Season with salt and pepper and roast cut side up on baking sheet until completely soft, about 1 hour. Let cool slightly and, with a fork, shred the squash flesh from the shell and transfer to a serving dish.

Meanwhile, in a food processor, pulse the pine nuts and basil to a paste. Add the butter and cheese and pulse to combine; season with salt and pepper.

Serve the squash warm with soft butter on the side to dollop on each serving.

1 large spaghetti squash (about 4 pounds)

Kosher salt and freshly cracked black pepper, to taste

1/4 cup pine nuts, toasted

8 large basil leaves, sliced

4 tablespoons unsalted butter, at room temperature

1/4 cup grated Pecorino Romano cheese plus more for serving

YIELD: 4 TO 6 SERVINGS

What makes this recipe really sing:
If you've never tried spaghetti squash, give it a go. It is easy to prepare; just roast it, scrape the flesh from the skin, and season it. You can even substitute this for real pasta—the delicious pesto-flavored butter melting into it is just the ticket.

What to toss in if you have it:
Spaghetti squash is rather mild in flavor, so you could add a small clove of minced garlic to the compound butter. The squash would be even tastier with some buttered toasted bread crumbs sprinkled over the top.

7.

Comfort à la CARTE

PASTA, POTATOES, AND OTHER PERFECT PLATE FILLERS

Does this chapter even need an introduction?
Every part of the globe has its own version of
stick-to-your-ribs goodness, and I've collected
some of my favorites to share with you. Nothing
says cozy-up like a side of Cheesy Penne or a
big heaping serving of Maple Whipped Sweet
Potatoes with Caramelized Onions. Kudos to all
the no-carb dieters out there, but I can't do it—
I need some comfort on my plate!

GERMAN POTATOES

1 1/2 pounds baby Yukon Gold potatoes, scrubbed and halved

Kosher salt and freshly cracked black pepper, to taste

4 slices smoked bacon

1/4 cup (about 6 to 8) cornichons or sweet baby gherkins, sliced

1/3 cup distilled white vinegar

1 tablespoon whole-grain mustard

YIELD: 4 SERVINGS

What makes this recipe really sing:
Bacon. Need I say more? This German staple is a great alternative to plain potato salad. The combination of salty bacon, tart white vinegar, and sweet gherkins is just delicious. Remember to dress the potatoes while they are still warm so they soak up the delicious dressing. Plus, you can take this to a picnic and not worry about its spoiling!

What to toss in if you have it:
Chop some shallots or red onion and throw them into the hot dressing; or for a fresh onion bite, slice 2 or 3 scallions and sprinkle them over the top before serving. These potatoes are also great with herbs—chop a mixture of basil and parsley and toss it in with the dressing.

Put the potatoes in a large pot, cover with water, salt generously, and bring to a boil over medium-high heat. Cook until fork-tender but not falling apart, 15 to 18 minutes. Drain and transfer to a large bowl.

Meanwhile, put the bacon in a skillet over medium heat. Cook until the bacon is crisp and the fat is rendered, about 6 minutes. Transfer the bacon to a paper towel–lined plate to drain. Add the cornichons, vinegar, and mustard to the skillet and bring to a simmer. Season with salt and pepper, reduce the heat to low, and keep warm while the potatoes cook.

Once the potatoes are drained, pour the hot dressing over them, season with salt and pepper, and toss well to coat. Crumble the bacon over the top and serve warm or at room temperature.

WALNUT-SAGE POTATO GRATIN

2 cups heavy cream

¾ cup walnuts, toasted and finely chopped

3 ½ pounds Yukon Gold potatoes, peeled and cut into ⅛-inch-thick slices

Kosher salt and freshly cracked black pepper, to taste

2 tablespoons roughly chopped fresh sage leaves

1 cup grated Gruyère cheese plus more for topping

YIELD: 4 TO 6 SERVINGS

What makes this recipe really sing:
The combination of walnuts and sage gives this comfort-food classic an earthy, nutty richness. The oils in the walnuts are released when the walnuts are toasted and heated in the cream, so the flavor permeates the whole dish. It's perfect for special occasions or to go alongside weeknight pork chops.

What to toss in if you have it:
A little garlic would taste great with this combination; simply smash a clove and rub the interior of the baking dish before assembly, then throw the clove in with the warming cream. You could also whisk 1 teaspoon of Dijon mustard into the cream mixture for a little tang.

Preheat the oven to 350°F.

In a saucepan over low heat, combine the cream and walnuts and bring to a simmer; keep the mixture warm over lowest heat while assembling the gratin.

In a 9 × 13-inch baking dish, arrange a third of the potato slices covering the bottom of the dish, overlapping slightly. Generously season with salt and pepper and sprinkle with a little sage, a third of the Gruyère, and a ladle of warmed walnut cream mixture. Repeat with another layer of potato, salt and pepper, sage, cheese, and cream mixture. Layer the remaining potatoes in straight, even rows over the top, season them, and then add the remaining sage and cream; finish with a scattering of cheese.

Cover with foil and bake 30 minutes. Reduce the oven temperature to 325°F and remove the foil. Continue to bake until the top is just starting to become golden, about 20 minutes more.

Remove from the oven and do your best to let the gratin rest 15 to 20 minutes before serving.

PARSNIP-POTATO MASH

Put the potatoes and parsnips in a large heavy-bottomed saucepan, cover with cold water, and salt generously. Bring the potatoes and parsnips to a boil over high heat; reduce heat to medium and simmer until fork-tender, 20 to 25 minutes. Put the butter and half-and-half in a small saucepan over medium-low heat until butter is melted and the mixture is hot.

Drain the potatoes and parsnips well and return them to the hot pan. Stir them in the pan to dry them out a bit. Add the hot butter and half-and-half, season with salt and pepper, and mash with a potato masher until smooth. Keep warm until ready to serve; garnish with chopped chives.

2 ½ pounds Yukon Gold potatoes, peeled and coarsely chopped

1 ½ pounds parsnips (about 8 small), peeled and chopped

Kosher salt and freshly cracked black pepper, to taste

¼ pound (1 stick) unsalted butter

¾ cup half-and-half

Finely chopped chives, for garnish (optional)

YIELD: 4 SERVINGS PLUS LEFTOVERS!

What makes this recipe really sing:
Parsnips are underutilized and underappreciated and they are so delicious! They add a great celery like sweetness to these mashed potatoes.

What to toss in if you have it:
Boil a couple of smashed garlic cloves along with the potatoes and parsnips; they will get super soft and mash beautifully. For a lighter version, cut the butter in half and replace the half-and-half with chicken broth.

RICOTTA-THYME SPAETZLE

Bring a large pot of salted water to a boil. Melt the butter in a large skillet; brush the interior of a large bowl with about 1 tablespoon butter and set the skillet with the butter aside while you make the dough.

Whisk the flour, salt, and pepper together in a large bowl. In a medium bowl, whisk the eggs and water well and fold in the ricotta and thyme leaves. Pour the wet ingredients into the flour and whisk well until smooth.

Holding a colander with medium holes over the boiling water, with a large rubber spatula, push the batter through the holes into the water in batches. Cook each batch until they all float, just 2 to 3 minutes. With a large strainer or slotted spoon, lift them out, shake off the excess water, and drop them into the buttered bowl. Continue cooking the dumplings, tossing them into the buttered bowl to keep them from sticking together.

Bring the remaining melted butter to a simmer over medium heat; cook until the butter begins to brown a bit (the milk solids will turn golden brown in the bottom of the skillet). Add the spaetzle, toss well to coat in the browned butter, and serve immediately.

Salt for the pot

4 tablespoons unsalted butter

2 cups unbleached all-purpose flour

Coarse salt and freshly ground black pepper, to taste

4 large eggs

3 tablespoons water

1 cup whole-milk ricotta cheese

1 tablespoon chopped fresh thyme leaves

YIELD: 4 SERVINGS

What makes this recipe really sing: Fresh ricotta adds a creaminess to these little dumplings; it's almost like having all the flavors of ravioli without all the fuss. Add to that the nutty flavor of browned butter and this deeply satisfying dish is perfect with chicken, pork, and even beef.

What to toss in if you have it: Folding in some fresh baby arugula leaves just before serving will add bright color and a bit of spicy bite to the spaetzle. Baby spinach leaves will work as well; you'll have a salad and side dish all on one plate.

This spaetzle is a super combo with the Pork Roast with Hard Cider Gravy on page 123.

THYME YORKSHIRE PUDDING

1 teaspoon kosher salt

1 cup unbleached all-purpose flour

1 ¼ cups whole milk, divided

3 large eggs, beaten

2 tablespoons chopped fresh thyme leaves

¼ cup olive oil or beef drippings from a roast

YIELD: 6 TO 8 SERVINGS

What makes this recipe really sing:

These are so easy to make and so impressive. They satisfy that craving for something starchy with a good roast meat, but are lighter and less filling than potatoes. Be sure to let the batter rest before baking them; they puff up into big, hollow pillows and are great for mopping up gravy!

What to toss in if you have it:

Whisk ½ teaspoon of ground dry mustard into the flour for a deeper flavor. You can also add some finely grated cheese, but not too much—the batter must be light enough to rise. These puddings are best with a beef roast or leg of lamb—use the drippings from the roasting pan to make the puddings with that much more flavor.

Sift the salt and the flour into a large bowl. Add half the milk and all the eggs to the flour mixture and whisk until smooth. Whisk in the remaining milk and then the thyme. Cover; let the batter sit at room temperature for at least 30 minutes, ideally 45 minutes.

Heat the oven to 450°F. Put a baking sheet on the bottom rack of the oven to catch any oil or batter drips.

Divide the ¼ cup oil among a 12-cup nonstick muffin tin or 12-hole Yorkshire pudding tray. Heat the muffin tin on the middle rack in the oven until the oil is almost smoking hot, about 10 minutes.

Uncover the batter and whisk one more time. Pour the batter into each cup, about three-quarters full. The batter will sizzle when being poured into the hot oil. Immediately place the muffin tin back into the oven. Bake in the oven for approximately 20 minutes, or until the puddings have risen and are golden brown in color. Turn the oven off and leave the puddings in the oven for just 5 more minutes to help set. Remove the puddings and serve while hot and puffed.

MAPLE WHIPPED SWEET POTATOES with CARAMELIZED ONIONS

4 large sweet potatoes, peeled and chopped into rough chunks

¼ cup plus 2 tablespoons pure grade B maple syrup

¼ cup extra-virgin olive oil, divided

2 teaspoons kosher salt plus more as needed

1 teaspoon freshly cracked black pepper plus more as needed

2 tablespoons unsalted butter

1 large Vidalia or other sweet onion, thinly sliced

YIELD: 4 SERVINGS

What makes this recipe really sing:
Sweet potatoes are so flavorful they don't need all that gooey marshmallow and brown sugar mess. Here's one spot where technique really makes a difference; cooking the onion until deep brown and caramelized adds another layer of complex sweetness that differs from the maple syrup.

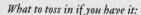

What to toss in if you have it:
A tablespoon or 2 of whole-grain Dijon mustard will add a savory tang; some grated Pecorino Romano will make the puree richer and give it a nutty undertone.

Preheat the oven to 375°F.

Put the sweet potatoes, ¼ cup maple syrup, 2 tablespoons olive oil, 2 teaspoons salt, and 1 teaspoon pepper in a large mixing bowl. Toss to evenly coat and transfer to a baking sheet; roast in the oven until the sweet potatoes are soft, 35 to 40 minutes. Check on them after 15 minutes and stir, if needed.

Meanwhile, melt the butter and 2 tablespoons olive oil together in a large skillet over medium-high heat. Add the sliced onion and 2 tablespoons maple syrup and season with salt and pepper, to taste. Cook, stirring frequently, until the onion is deep golden brown, about 10 minutes, adding water, a tablespoon at a time, if the skillet gets too dry. Remove from the heat and set aside.

Transfer the sweet potatoes to a food processor and add a tablespoon of hot water. Pulse until just blended and then add half the caramelized onion. Pulse a few more seconds to incorporate the onion; for a very smooth puree, add another tablespoon of water and run the machine for 1 minute. Fold in the remaining caramelized onion, reserving some for garnish.

Serve in a warm dish and garnish with the reserved caramelized onion.

CHEESY PENNE

Salt for the pot

1 pound fresh or dried penne pasta

1/2 cup whole milk

2 teaspoons Dijon mustard

3/4 cup heavy cream

4 ounces aged English white cheddar cheese, grated

Kosher salt and freshly cracked black pepper, to taste

YIELD: 4 SERVINGS

What makes this recipe really sing:
Although it can be tricky to find, I really love using fresh penne pasta for this dish. It has a really satisfying, toothsome, chewy texture that is great with the cheesy sauce. Adding Dijon mustard gives this easy "uber mac-and-cheese" a spicy, vinegary kick.

What to toss in if you have it:
Sauté some fresh bread crumbs from a brioche loaf or baguette in a little butter and sprinkle the crunchy golden crumbs over the penne just before serving. You can also toss in some diced turkey or ham and cooked broccoli for a one-dish meal.

Bring a large saucepan of salted water to a boil over high heat. Add the pasta; cook until al dente, according to package instructions, and drain. Return the pasta to the saucepan.

Whisk the milk with the Dijon mustard in a small bowl and add to the pot with cooked pasta, along with the cream and grated cheddar. Stir over medium-low heat until the cheese melts and the mixture is nice and thick. Season with salt and pepper and serve immediately.

CLASSIC BOURBON BAKED BEANS

In a bowl, whisk together the brown sugar, tomato paste, mustard, water, and bourbon until the sugar is dissolved. Drain the beans and put them in a large heavy-bottomed stock pot or Dutch oven. Pour the sauce mixture over them, stir to combine, and bring the beans to a simmer over medium heat, stirring frequently. Reduce the heat to low to maintain a gentle simmer. Cover and cook the beans, stirring every 10 to 15 minutes, until the beans are soft and the sauce is very thick, about 4 hours.

If the beans get too dry, add more water, ½ cup at a time. Once the beans are soft, season them with salt and pepper and keep cooking, covered, an additional 30 minutes. If the beans are too wet and runny, remove the lid and cook, stirring often, until desired consistency is reached. Serve warm or at room temperature.

1 cup packed dark brown sugar

¼ cup tomato paste

½ cup spicy Dijon mustard

1 cup water plus more, as needed

½ cup bourbon

1 pound dried navy beans, soaked in a large bowl of water overnight

Kosher salt and freshly cracked black pepper, to taste

YIELD: 8 SERVINGS

What makes this recipe really sing:
Take the time to make beans from scratch; using soaked dried beans results in much firmer texture and the beans hold their shape better than precooked canned beans. This mix of sweet, spicy, and boozy will be a new classic recipe for your file.

What to toss in if you have it:
Dice up 4 ounces of slab bacon and cook it until crisp in the pot; remove all but a couple of tablespoons of the bacon grease and proceed with the recipe. You can also add chopped onions and a can of minced chipotle chili if you like your beans really spicy.

STONE-GROUND GRITS
with GRUYÈRE

1 cup stone-ground white corn grits (I use Falls Mill and store in freezer.)

2 cups chicken stock plus more if needed

2 cups half-and-half

1 cup grated Gruyère cheese

Kosher salt and freshly cracked black pepper, to taste

YIELD: 4 SERVINGS

What makes this recipe really sing:

Using really good-quality freshly ground corn is the key to the best grits. There are grist mills around the country that sell their grits online; be sure to store grits in the freezer, though, as they can spoil easily at room temperature.

What to toss in if you have it:

You can substitute other sharp cheeses, such as aged white cheddar, or a triple-cream cheese for even richer grits. These are fantastic for breakfast; crumble some cooked spicy breakfast sausage into the grits and top them with a fried egg.

Put the grits in a large bowl, fill it with water, and stir. Using a slotted spoon, skim the floating bran off the top; strain the water and discard.

Bring the stock and half-and-half to a boil in a medium heavy-bottomed pan and slowly whisk in the grits. Reduce the heat to medium-low and cook, stirring often, until thick and creamy, about 45 minutes. If the grits get too thick, stir in additional hot stock or water to loosen and thin them.

Stir in the Gruyère until melted, season with salt and pepper, and serve immediately.

WILD RICE CASSEROLE

1 cup uncooked wild rice

1 small orange or yellow bell pepper, seeded and finely diced

1 cup frozen pearl onions, thawed

2 large eggs

1/2 cup grated Parmesan cheese plus more as needed

Kosher salt and freshly cracked black pepper, to taste

YIELD: 4 SERVINGS

What makes this recipe really sing:
I love the texture of wild rice; it never gets mushy and is a great starch to add all kinds of foods to. This casserole is really comforting and filling and a great alternative to mashed potatoes with your next roasted chicken.

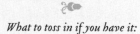

What to toss in if you have it:
Wild rice will stand up to crunchy textures; try adding some toasted chopped hazelnuts and a drizzle of hazelnut oil to the mixture before baking. A sprinkling of some sliced scallions at the table will add a nice green color and fresh onion bite.

Cook the rice according to package instructions; drain and cool to room temperature.

Preheat the oven to 350°F.

Put the rice in a mixing bowl; add the pepper, onions, eggs, cheese, and salt and pepper and mix until well combined. Transfer the mixture to a 1-quart baking dish and sprinkle a generous handful of Parmesan over the top. Bake until set and golden brown on top, 35 to 40 minutes. Let stand 10 minutes before serving.

TOMATO RICE
with MUSTARD SEEDS

Heat ¼ cup oil in a saucepan with a lid over medium heat. Add the mustard seeds and cook, swirling the pan, until they begin to pop and turn gray. (You may need to hold the lid over the pan as they tend to pop like popcorn.) Add the rice and stir until it is coated in oil and begins to turn translucent, 2 to 3 minutes.

Carefully add the tomato puree and water and season the rice with salt and pepper. Bring to a boil, reduce the heat to low, cover, and cook until rice completely absorbs the liquid, 12 to 14 minutes. Once the liquid is evaporated, turn off the heat, leave the lid on the pan, and let the rice stand for at least 10 minutes.

Meanwhile, heat the 2 tablespoons oil in a small skillet over medium-high heat. Add the shallot rounds and stir-fry quickly until golden brown. Drain on a paper towel–lined plate and season with salt.

To serve, fluff the rice with a fork and turn out onto a serving platter. Scatter the fried shallot rounds over the top and serve immediately.

¼ cup plus 2 tablespoons canola or vegetable oil

2 tablespoons red mustard seeds

1 cup basmati rice

1 ½ cups tomato puree

1 cup water

Kosher salt and freshly cracked black pepper, to taste

1 shallot, thinly sliced into rounds

YIELD: 4 SERVINGS

What makes this recipe really sing:
This rice employs a technique used in Indian cooking, when the spices are "bloomed," or toasted, before they are added to the other ingredients. This releases all of the oils in the spices and develops deeper flavor. The crunchy browned shallot rounds are a great little garnish to add to any rice dish or vegetable.

What to toss in if you have it:
Finely dice some peeled carrot and add it with the tomato puree and water. You can also stir in some frozen peas at the end of cooking to make a nice Indian-style rice side dish for fish or chicken.

RICH PORCINI MUSHROOM RISOTTO

1 ounce dried porcini mushrooms

5 cups boiling water

4 tablespoons unsalted butter

1 1/2 cups Arborio rice

1 cup dry white wine

1/2 cup grated Pecorino Romano cheese plus more for serving

Kosher salt and freshly cracked black pepper, to taste

YIELD: 4 SERVINGS

What makes this recipe really sing:

Dried mushrooms are an absolute must in any pantry. Here I use porcini, which have a deep, rich, earthy flavor even more pronounced than fresh mushrooms. Dried mushrooms must always be soaked, but NEVER throw out the liquid you soak them in—it is loaded with flavor and can be used, as I do here, as a stock for the risotto. Just be sure to let the sediment settle before you pour the mushroom liquid off, leaving it behind.

What to toss in if you have it:

For an even richer risotto, use low-sodium chicken or beef stock instead of water. Some sliced baby asparagus would be both pretty and delicious in this recipe; just toss it in during the last addition of broth so it cooks but is still crisp-tender.

Put the mushrooms in a bowl and pour the boiling water over them. Let stand 15 minutes until the mushrooms are very soft; with a slotted spoon, remove them from the liquid, coarsely chop, and reserve. Carefully pour the mushroom liquid into a saucepan, making sure to leave any sediment in the bowl. Heat the mushroom liquid over medium heat until hot but not boiling.

In a large saucepan or deep skillet, melt the butter over medium heat. Continue cooking, stirring occasionally, until the milk solids begin to brown lightly; add the rice and stir until the butter has turned golden brown. Add the chopped mushrooms and wine and bring to a simmer; cook until the wine is nearly evaporated.

While stirring constantly, add the hot mushroom broth, a half cup at a time, allowing the rice to absorb the liquid completely before adding more. Once all of the broth has been added, stir in 1/2 cup cheese. Taste and adjust seasoning; serve immediately and pass additional cheese at the table.

CORNBREAD DRESSING

Preheat the oven to 375°F.

In a large skillet over medium heat, melt 2 tablespoons butter and add the onion, seasoning with salt and pepper. Cook, stirring often, until light golden, 6 to 8 minutes; remove from the skillet. Raise the heat to medium-high and add the water, scraping up the brown bits from the bottom and allowing water to simmer just a couple of minutes to infuse in the onion flavor and remove from the heat.

Put the cornbread in a large mixing bowl. Melt the remaining 6 tablespoons butter in a small pan over medium heat and let bubble until the milk solids start to turn golden. Add the sage leaves as soon as butter starts to turn color and briefly fry until beginning to crisp, about 30 seconds. With a slotted spoon, remove the sage and place it on top of the cornbread to drain and crisp; remove the butter from the heat. Add the eggs and cooked onion to the cornbread and pour the browned butter over the mix. Season with salt and pepper; add the onion-infused water, 1 tablespoon at a time, gently folding, until the cornbread is evenly moistened but not soggy. Pour the dressing into a 9 × 11-inch baking dish and bake until the top is golden brown in color and the dressing is set in the middle, about 30 minutes.

¼ pound (1 stick) unsalted butter, divided

1 large Vidalia or Spanish onion, chopped (about 1 cup)

Kosher salt and freshly cracked black pepper, to taste

¾ cup water

6 cups cubed (1-inch pieces) store-bought or homemade cornbread (about 1 pound)

⅓ cup fresh sage leaves (about 12), stems removed

2 large eggs, beaten

YIELD: 6 TO 8 SERVINGS

What makes this recipe really sing:
This recipe is all about utilizing cooking technique to get the maximum flavor from just a few ingredients. Browning the butter adds a nutty, rich roundness; frying the sage brings out the herb's natural oils and adds some crunchy bits to the dressing, and caramelizing the onion adds depth and sweetness to the dressing.

What to toss in if you have it:
Dressings are great for incorporating your favorite flavors. This one would be tasty with some browned maple sausage and diced crisp apple, or you could go southern and add chopped country ham and sliced celery.

TOASTED FRUITY ISRAELI COUSCOUS

2 tablespoons lemon-flavored olive oil plus more as needed

2 cups Israeli couscous

¼ cup roasted shelled unsalted pistachios, coarsely chopped

2 ¼ cups hot water

Kosher salt and freshly cracked black pepper, to taste

6 dried Turkish apricots, chopped

2 scallions, sliced

YIELD: 4 SERVINGS

What makes this recipe really sing:
Flavored olive oils really come in handy to add punch to side dishes, salads, and appetizers. Here the lemon olive oil, paired with apricots and pistachios, gives this dish a wonderful Mediterranean twist. This is a simple dish to make and can liven up any humdrum weeknight meal.

What to toss in if you have it:
To take the exotic flavors even further, add a ½ teaspoon curry powder to the water when cooking the couscous. Toss in some shredded leftover chicken and serve it on a bed of greens for a quick meal in itself.

Heat the olive oil in a saucepan over medium heat. Add the couscous and pistachios and cook, stirring, until toasted and light golden brown, about 10 minutes. Add the water, season with salt and pepper, and bring to a boil; reduce the heat to a simmer, cover, and cook until the liquid is absorbed, about 10 minutes.

Remove the lid, stir in the apricots and scallions, taste, and adjust the seasoning. Serve warm with a little more lemon olive oil drizzled over the top, if desired.

8.

Sweet
ENDINGS

WRAP IT ALL UP WITH DESSERT

Dessert might be the hardest thing to pull
off in five ingredients, but I've learned that with
the sweet stuff it's all about technique, technique,
technique. What I love most is figuring out
how to unlock the natural sweetness in my
ingredients—pineapples, for example—and
work it to my advantage. Here you'll find simple
recipes with big results, perfect for the sweet
tooth in all of us.

CHAI-SPICED S'MORES

8 ounces bittersweet chocolate, finely chopped

¾ cup heavy cream

1 tablespoon loose chai tea leaves

16 honey graham cracker squares (2 ½-inch square)

1 ½ cups mini marshmallows or 16 jumbo marshmallows

SPECIAL EQUIPMENT:
8 metal skewers

YIELD: 4 SERVINGS (8 S'MORES)

What makes this recipe really sing:
Truly a favorite dessert, my recipe is a grown-up version with dark chocolate and warm chai spices; adding tea to this classic adds an elegant twist.

What to toss in if you have it:
Try using different tea leaves such as Earl Grey with the cream, which will add a light smokiness. Tea and chocolate are a match made in heaven.

Set an oven rack 6 to 8 inches from the broiler and preheat broiler.

Put the chocolate in a heat-proof bowl.

Put the cream in a small saucepan and bring to a simmer over medium heat. Add the tea leaves, stir, remove from the heat, and let stand 10 minutes. Return the tea-infused cream to medium heat until just simmering. Pour the cream through a fine-mesh strainer set over the bowl of chocolate. Shake the bowl to evenly distribute the cream and let stand 5 minutes to melt the chocolate. Stir until very smooth and cool the chocolate to room temperature. Discard the tea leaves.

Put 8 graham cracker squares on a baking sheet and spread ½ teaspoon of cooled chocolate on each. Arrange the mini marshmallows on the chocolate, covering each graham cracker square completely. Transfer the baking sheet to the broiler and toast the marshmallows until deep golden brown, about 1 minute. (DO NOT leave the oven; keep an eye on the marshmallows—they toast very quickly.)

Remove the s'mores from the oven and put about 1 teaspoon chocolate in the center of each on top of the browned marshmallow. Top each with a second graham cracker square, pressing lightly to spread the chocolate to the edges. Let cool a minute or two before devouring.

To make s'mores the old-fashioned way: Spread ½ teaspoon chocolate on each of 8 graham cracker squares (the bottoms of the s'mores); dollop a teaspoon of chocolate onto the center of the remaining 8 squares (the tops). Put 2 jumbo marshmallows on each skewer and toast them over an open flame until browned (or charred) as desired. Transfer the toasted marshmallows from each skewer onto the center of a bottom graham cracker square. Invert a graham cracker top over the marshmallows and press lightly while you simultaneously pull the skewer from the marshmallows to create a sandwich.

Note: *Unused chocolate chai sauce can be stored in an airtight container in the refrigerator for up to 1 week. It can be melted and poured over ice cream or stirred into hot milk for chai-spiced hot chocolate.*

MOCHA MERINGUE BARK

½ cup blanched slivered almonds, divided

1 teaspoon plus ¼ cup granulated sugar

4 egg whites

Pinch of salt

1 tablespoon instant espresso powder

⅓ cup mini chocolate chips

YIELD: 4 TO 6 SERVINGS

What makes this recipe really sing:
Meringues are a wonderful, crunchy treat (with no fat!) that are great for satisfying a craving for a little sweet bite. This version combines the flavor of coffee and chocolate for a perfect afternoon pick-me-up.

What to toss in if you have it:
If you like the flavor of cinnamon in your lattes, add ¼ teaspoon ground cinnamon to the sugar and almonds before pulsing in a food processor. A little more can be gently sprinkled over the meringue after it has been spread on the baking sheet.

Preheat the oven to 250°F.

Line a rimmed baking sheet with a silicone baking mat or parchment paper.

Put ¼ cup blanched almonds and 1 teaspoon sugar into a food processor and pulse until it resembles cornmeal; reserve. Finely chop the remaining almonds.

In a stand mixer with the whisk attachment, beat the egg whites and salt until very soft peaks have formed. In a small bowl, stir together ¼ cup sugar and the espresso powder. With the mixer running on low, slowly add in the sugar and espresso powder, 1 tablespoon at a time, whipping just to a stiff peak (do not overbeat). Gently fold in the reserved almond flour.

With a large offset spatula, spread the meringue batter on the lined baking sheet in an even layer, about ½-inch thick. Sprinkle the finely chopped almonds and chocolate chips evenly over the surface of the meringue; bake for 1 hour and turn the oven off, leaving the meringue in the oven to dry out further and cool for an additional 1 hour.

To serve, break the meringue into pieces.

Note: *Leftover meringue can be stored in an airtight container at room temperature in a dry cool place for up to 3 days. If the meringue gets chewy, put it back into a 200°F oven for about 30 minutes, turn off the oven, and let it dry inside the oven while it cools.*

FROZEN LEMON WHIP
with BLUEBERRY SAUCE

Line a 6-cup jumbo muffin tin with paper muffin liners.

Whisk together the egg yolks and sugar until well combined and add the lemon juice and zest. Pour into a heavy-bottomed saucepan and cook over medium-low heat, stirring constantly, until the mixture thickens to the consistency of gravy, 8 to 10 minutes (it should cling to the spoon when you stop stirring). Pour the mixture through a fine-mesh sieve placed over a large glass bowl; stir the mixture occasionally to help release some of the heat. Once it has cooled to room temperature, put plastic wrap directly on the surface of the lemon curd to prevent a skin from forming and refrigerate until firm.

Whip the heavy cream to soft peaks. Whisk the chilled lemon curd to loosen it and fold half the cream into it to lighten; gently fold in remaining whipped cream until just blended. Divide the lemon whip among the muffin cups, smoothing the tops. Put the muffin tin on a sheet tray, cover with plastic wrap, and freeze for at least 4 hours.

To serve, remove the muffin tin from the freezer and let stand 10 minutes. Serve immediately by placing thin lemon slices on 6 plates and on each plate inverting a lemon whip directly on top of the lemon slices (this prevents its sliding on the plate). Drizzle blueberry sauce over the tops and around the frozen lemon whips and top with a few blueberries. Enjoy your refreshing cold treat!

For the Blueberry Sauce: Put the blueberries in a small saucepan with the sugar, lemon zest, and lemon juice. Bring to a simmer over medium heat and cook, stirring, until the sugar dissolves and the berries begin to burst. Place in a blender and puree, then strain through a fine-mesh sieve over a glass bowl and chill, covered, in the refrigerator until ready to use.

6 large egg yolks

1/2 cup granulated sugar

1/2 cup freshly squeezed lemon juice, zest of 3 lemons, and thin lemon slices for serving

2 cups heavy cream

Fresh blueberries, for serving

BLUEBERRY SAUCE:

2 cups fresh blueberries plus more for garnish

1/4 cup granulated sugar

Zest of 1 lemon plus 1/4 cup freshly squeezed lemon juice

YIELD: 6 SERVINGS

What makes this recipe really sing:
Tart lemon curd is a great thing to have on hand and pairing it with blueberries is a classic combination. Store-bought curd is expensive and sometimes has additives—make my homemade version for the truest lemon flavor.

What to toss in if you have it:
Fresh ginger is a natural partner to lemon; peel and finely grate a 4-inch piece of ginger into a bowl. Using a spoon or your fingers, squeeze the juice from the ginger and add it to the lemon juice before making the curd. It will add a surprising warm roundness to this delicious frozen treat.

ROASTED PINEAPPLE
with THYME-GINGER ICE

1 teaspoon thyme leaves plus
small sprigs for garnish

Two 12-ounce bottles ginger beer
or all-natural ginger soda

1 whole pineapple, peeled,
eyes removed, and sliced into
8 even slices

Vegetable oil

1 tablespoon granulated sugar

Kosher salt, to taste

YIELD: 4 SERVINGS

What makes this recipe really sing:
Ginger beer is very spicy and the
spiciness is enhanced when it's frozen.
It's a great counterpart to the sweet,
caramel flavor of the roasted pineapple.
For milder ice, use natural ginger ale
or ginger soda.

What to toss in if you have it:
Sprinkle finely chopped smoked
almonds over the dessert—the flavor
will enhance the sweet and spicy
elements of this uber-healthy dessert.

Scatter the thyme leaves among the compartments of two large ice
cube trays; fill the trays with ginger beer and freeze at least 6 hours and
preferably overnight.

Preheat the oven to 400°F.

Put the pineapple slices on a nonstick baking sheet. Brush both sides
very lightly with vegetable oil and sprinkle them evenly with the sugar;
sprinkle very lightly with salt as well. Roast in the oven 20 minutes;
remove and flip the slices. Continue roasting until they turn golden,
about 10 minutes more. Remove them from oven and cool slightly on
the baking sheet.

Transfer the ginger-beer ice cubes to a food processor and pulse until
broken down and fluffy. Transfer to a small cake pan or baking dish.
Use immediately or freeze until ready to serve.

To serve, put a slice of warm pineapple on each of four dessert plates, top
it with a scoop of ginger ice, and garnish it with a small sprig of thyme.

Note: *If you're not using the ginger ice immediately, refreeze it. To loosen it,
scrape it with a heavy fork until fluffy.*

WHITE CHOCOLATE MOUSSE

7 ounces white chocolate, very finely chopped

2 large egg yolks

2 tablespoons granulated sugar

1 ¼ cups heavy cream, divided

12 fresh blackberries, for garnish

YIELD: 4 SERVINGS

What makes this recipe really sing:
This is a real French-style mousse made with egg yolks and cream. When properly made, it should be as smooth as silk in your mouth. Just be sure to work slowly while pouring the hot milk on the yolks so they don't heat too fast and scramble.

What to toss in if you have it:
Throw a couple of rinsed whole mint sprigs into the cream while it is heating, then strain them out when you pour the mixture over the chocolate. The oils from the herb will bring a fresh, minty undertone to the mousse.

Put the white chocolate in a large glass bowl and set aside.

Whisk the egg yolks and sugar together in a small bowl until pale in color.

In a saucepan, over medium-low heat, bring ¼ cup cream to a simmer. While whisking, slowly pour the cream into the yolk and sugar mixture to temper. Pour the creamy mixture back into the saucepan, return to medium-low heat, and stir with a wooden spoon until thickened and it coats the back of the spoon.

Pour the hot egg mixture through a fine-mesh sieve placed directly over the chopped chocolate. Let stand a few minutes without disturbing and then stir the chocolate until completely smooth.

In another bowl, whip the remaining 1 cup cream until soft peaks form. Fold half the whipped cream into the white chocolate mix to lighten and then fold in the remaining whipped cream.

Spoon the white chocolate mousse into four serving cups and refrigerate until set, approximately 1 hour.

Garnish each serving with 3 blackberries and serve.

PROSECCO GELATIN PARFAIT

Put the prosecco, ½ cup sugar, and water in a saucepan and bring to a boil. Reduce the heat to a simmer and cook for 5 minutes to burn off some of the alcohol. Remove from the heat and slowly whisk in the gelatin until completely dissolved. Pour into a 9 × 11-inch baking dish, cool to room temperature, then place in the refrigerator to set for at least 4 hours.

Whip the cream to medium stiff peaks. Whisk the remaining ¼ cup sugar into the mascarpone until smooth. Add a third of the whipped cream to the mascarpone to lighten and then fold in remaining whipped cream.

To serve, cut the prosecco gelatin into 1 × 1-inch cubes and put a layer into the bottoms of four parfait glasses. Divide half of the cream mixture among the glasses on top of the gelatin and then repeat two more layers, ending with a final dollop of cream. Put in a long spoon and dig in!

One (750-ml) bottle prosecco

¾ cup granulated sugar, divided

½ cup water

Two ¼-ounce packets
unflavored gelatin

1 cup heavy cream

½ pint mascarpone cheese,
at room temperature

YIELD: 4 TO 6 SERVINGS

What makes this recipe really sing:
Who hasn't had gelatin in some form or another at least once in their lives? I used to love those pretty layered, tall glasses at the diner as a kid, so I found a way to make a grown-up version. The sparkling wine is an adult twist on the lime and strawberry versions, making this parfait worthy of any fine restaurant.

What to toss in if you have it:
Look for golden raspberries in the farmer's market in the late spring. Gently stir them into the cooled gelatin before chilling it; they'll give the gelatin a burst of fresh, juicy berry flavor and look lovely suspended in the golden gelatin.

HAZELNUT AFFOGATO SUNDAE

With a whisk or handheld mixer, whip the cream in a bowl until very thick but still liquid; while whisking constantly, add the Frangelico and whip until soft peaks form.

To serve, place 2 scoops gelato into each of four dessert bowls. Sprinkle a tablespoon of hazelnuts over the gelato and top with a dollop of flavored whipped cream. Rub ½ an amaretti cookie along a fine grater over the whipped cream to garnish. Serve immediately.

1 pint heavy whipping cream

1 ½ tablespoons Frangelico

1 pint espresso gelato

¼ cup blanched hazelnuts, toasted

2 amaretti cookies (I love the cute wrapped Lazzaroni cookies.)

YIELD: 4 SERVINGS

What makes this recipe really sing:
A true affogato is hot espresso poured over a scoop of ice cream. I bring the flavor of hazelnuts and almonds together here with Frangelico, a hazelnut liqueur, and amaretti cookies, which have amaretto, or almond liqueur in them.

What to toss in if you have it:
If you have an espresso maker, make the sundae in a glass and pour a shot of hot espresso over the gelato. Hot, cold, crunchy, creamy, sweet— a perfect dessert!

MILLIONAIRE'S SHORTBREAD

SHORTBREAD:

1/2 pound (2 sticks) unsalted butter, cut into small pieces plus more for greasing the pans

2 cups unbleached all-purpose flour plus more for preparing the pans

2/3 cup granulated sugar

1/2 teaspoon kosher salt

CARAMEL LAYER:

Two 14-ounce cans sweetened condensed milk

2 tablespoons unsalted butter

CHOCOLATE TOPPING:

12 ounces good-quality milk chocolate, chopped

Fleur de sel or flaky sea salt, for garnish

YIELD: 32 PIECES

What makes this recipe really sing:
Crunchy, rich shortbread with caramel and chocolate? Heaven. A sprinkle of salt, preferably French or gray sea salt, over the top really brings it to life. You'll be glad this recipe makes two pans!

What to toss in if you have it:
Shortbread is as good as the butter you put in it. Splurge on a high-end Irish or French butter for the shortbread and bittersweet chocolate for the topping for a decadent touch. Some finely chopped toasted almonds in the shortbread crust will add even more crunch.

For the shortbread: Preheat the oven to 350°F.

Butter two 8-inch-square nonstick pans and coat with flour, tapping off the excess. Place the flour, sugar, and salt in a food processor and pulse once. Add the butter and pulse until the mixture resembles peas. Press the shortbread mixture into the prepared pans and bake until golden brown around the edges, about 20 minutes. Remove from the oven and let cool completely.

For the caramel layer: In a heavy-bottomed saucepan over medium-low heat, combine the condensed milk and 2 tablespoons butter. Slowly bring the mixture to a boil, stirring continuously. Continue stirring over the heat until the mixture becomes thick and amber in color, 15 to 20 minutes. Pour the caramel over the shortbread and spread evenly using an offset spatula. Cool to room temperature.

For the chocolate topping: In a glass bowl set over a saucepan of simmering water, melt the chocolate. Once the chocolate has melted, pour it over the cooled caramel layer. Sprinkle a little fleur de sel over the surface of the chocolate to garnish. Cool at room temperature for about 10 minutes and then place in the refrigerator to set completely. Cut into 2-inch squares and serve.

CHOCOLATE POTS DE CRÈME with CHERRY WHIP

4 ounces good-quality bittersweet chocolate, chopped

2 cups heavy cream, divided

¼ cup plus 1 teaspoon granulated sugar

2 large egg yolks

¼ cup cherry preserves or jam

SPECIAL EQUIPMENT:

9-inch removable-bottomed fluted tart pan

YIELD: 4 SERVINGS

What makes this recipe really sing:
The beauty of custards is that they normally don't have any flour, so the texture is silky smooth from the eggs and cream. Make sure the cream is very hot when being added to the chocolate and keep stirring until smooth, when there are no longer any visible chocolate bits.

What to toss in if you have it:
Chocolate can be paired with many flavors; the addition of a little liqueur, spices, or coffee brings out even more chocolate flavor. Try adding 1 teaspoon of instant espresso powder, if you have some, to the hot cream. It will add even more depth and richness to the pots de crème.

Preheat the oven to 350°F.

Bring a kettle of water to a boil.

Put the chocolate into a heat-proof bowl. Heat 1½ cups cream and ¼ cup sugar, whisking until just simmering and the sugar is dissolved. Pour the hot cream over the chocolate and whisk until the chocolate is melted and smooth. Put the yolks in a small bowl; while whisking, add a small amount of the warm chocolate mixture to temper the yolks. Whisk the yolk mixture into the chocolate until well combined. Transfer the mixture to a liquid measuring cup for easy pouring.

Put four 6-ounce ramekins into a high-sided baking dish. Evenly fill the ramekins with the chocolate mixture; carefully fill the baking dish with hot water until it reaches halfway up the sides of the ramekins and transfer the baking dish to the oven. Bake until the custards are set but still jiggle slightly in the center, about 30 minutes. Remove the baking dish from the oven and carefully transfer the custards to a rack and cool to room temperature. Refrigerate the custards at least 2 hours and preferably overnight.

When ready to serve, whisk the cherry preserves in a small bowl until loosened and thin. In another bowl with a clean whisk, whip the remaining ½ cup cream and 1 teaspoon sugar until firm peaks form; gently fold the whipped cream into the cherry preserves until just combined and streaky. Serve the pots de crème chilled, topped with dollops of cherry whipped cream.

GINGER PUMPKIN TART

2 ½ cups crushed thin Swedish ginger cookie crumbs, (about 55 to 60 cookies)

6 tablespoons unsalted butter, melted

One 15-ounce can pumpkin puree, preferably organic

¾ cup sweetened condensed milk

2 large egg yolks

Pinch of salt

SPECIAL EQUIPMENT:
9-inch removable-bottomed fluted tart pan

YIELD: 6 TO 8 SERVINGS

What makes this recipe really sing:
Classic desserts are tricky with just a few ingredients, but this one will blow you away. It has the satisfying pumpkin flavor and richness of a pie with the zip of ginger in the crust.

❧

What to toss in if you have it:
A pinch of cinnamon and freshly grated nutmeg in the filling will enhance the pumpkin, and some finely ground almonds in the crust will give the tart a crunchier texture. Of course, a dollop of softly whipped cream with some vanilla extract in it never hurt any tart or pie!

❧

Preheat the oven to 350°F.

Put a 9-inch removable-bottomed fluted tart pan on a baking sheet.

Make the crust by combining the cookie crumbs with the melted butter until well blended. Pour the butter-coated crumbs into the tart pan evenly and press over the bottom and up the sides of the pan with the bottom of a measuring cup. Bake until set and a bit darker in color, 10 to 12 minutes; remove from the oven and set aside to cool.

In a bowl, whisk together the pumpkin, condensed milk, yolks, and salt until well blended. Pour the filling into the cooled crust, return it to the oven, and bake until set and beginning to brown on the top, about 30 minutes. Remove the tart from the oven, cool to room temperature, and then chill in the refrigerator, at least 1 hour or until ready to serve.

To serve, carefully remove outer tart shell ring and slice. Eat and enjoy!

Note: *Any crushed gingersnap cookie will do; just be sure to use 2 ½ cups of crumbs for the crust.*

BANANAS FOSTER

Combine the butter, sugar, and cinnamon in a skillet and cook over low heat, stirring to dissolve sugar. Add the bananas and cook to soften, while basting them with the syrup in the skillet. Remove the skillet from the heat and add the rum; return the skillet to the heat, tipping it to ignite the alcohol. If you have an electric stove, ignite the liquor with a long match or lighter.

Once the flame has burned out, serve the bananas in shallow bowls, 4 pieces per person, and spoon the sauce over them.

4 tablespoons salted butter

1 cup dark brown sugar

¾ teaspoon ground cinnamon

4 bananas, cut in half and then in half lengthwise

⅓ cup dark rum

YIELD: 4 SERVINGS

What makes this recipe really sing:
Having spent some of my childhood in New Orleans, I find this classic dish reminds me of home. It is so easy to make and has really impressive, simple flavors that just seem to make a banana lover out of almost anyone.

What to toss in if you have it:
Bananas Foster is classically served as a topping for vanilla ice cream, but I do love it on its own. Try butter pecan or chocolate ice cream for a twist or even adding your favorite toasted chopped nut. Traditionally, banana liqueur is used and is a great addition or, if you are a coconut lover, try this with coconut rum instead.

POACHED PEARS with CREAMY PECAN SAUCE

For the poached pears: In a large pot, combine the water and sugar over medium-high heat. Using a vegetable peeler, pull wide strips of lemon zest from the lemon and add to the pot along with the juice of the whole lemon. Bring to a boil, stirring to dissolve the sugar; reduce the heat to maintain a gentle simmer. Submerge the pears in the simmering liquid, adding more water if necessary to just cover the pears. Cut a piece of parchment paper into a circle just large enough to cover the pot. Ease the paper down into the pot until it is touching the surface of the liquid. Simmer the pears for about 30 minutes, or until a knife inserted directly into a pear meets little resistance. Remove from the heat and cool the pears completely in the poaching liquid.

For the creamy pecan sauce: In a saucepan, combine the brown sugar and water and bring to a boil. Reduce the heat to medium and simmer until the sauce is reduced and thicker and takes on a dark golden brown color, 8 to 10 minutes. Carefully stir in the cream, reduce the heat to medium-low, and simmer until very thick, 2 to 3 minutes more. Stir in the toasted pecans and salt.

Serve 1 to 2 pear halves per person, drizzled with the creamy pecan sauce.

POACHED PEARS:

5 cups of water plus more as needed

1/2 cup packed light brown sugar

1 lemon

6 ripe but firm pears, such as Bosc or Anjou, peeled, halved lengthwise, and cored

CREAMY PECAN SAUCE:

3/4 cup packed light brown sugar

1/2 cup water

1/2 cup heavy cream

1 cup pecan halves, toasted

Pinch of kosher salt

YIELD: 6 TO 12 SERVINGS

What makes this recipe really sing:
Pears are naturally very sweet but sometimes there just isn't time to let them ripen completely. Have no fear—poaching a firm pear is the answer. In fact, even if the pears feel like rocks, the hot poaching liquid will penetrate their flesh and soften them without turning them to mush.

What to toss in if you have it:
Poaching liquid can be flavored with just about anything. Add a cup of sparkling wine or champagne for an elegant flavor. A scraped vanilla bean or a few slices of fresh ginger can really perk up the flavors as the pears poach.

FLOURLESS CHOCOLATE-LOVER'S CAKE

¼ pound (1 stick) unsalted butter plus more for greasing the pan

6 ounces bittersweet dark chocolate

5 large eggs, at room temperature

¾ cup plus 2 tablespoons dark (at least 70 percent) cocoa powder

1 cup heavy cream

YIELD: 10 TO 12 SERVINGS

What makes this recipe really sing:
Using great-quality cocoa powder is the key here. This dessert is gluten free, and is incredibly easy and super fast to whip together. This will satisfy the chocolate lover in the house…you'll be hard pressed to find a more intense chocolate dessert anywhere.

What to toss in if you have it:
Coffee is a great addition to chocolate desserts; it deepens the flavor. Add a teaspoon of instant espresso powder to the melting chocolate. Or, for a Mexican spin, add ½ teaspoon cinnamon to the cake batter and dust the top of the cake with more before serving.

Preheat the oven to 375°F.

Butter and parchment line a 9-inch round baking pan.

Roughly chop the chocolate and place it in a bowl over a pan of simmering water but not directly touching it. Add the butter and melt until smooth. Meanwhile, whisk the eggs in a bowl until slightly frothy. Remove the chocolate from the heat and whisk a small amount into the eggs; pour the eggs into the chocolate and whisk until combined. Using a rubber spatula, fold ¾ cup cocoa powder until just incorporated and pour into the prepared pan. Bake 25 to 30 minutes, until crust on top of cake forms.

While cake is baking, pour the cream and 2 tablespoons cocoa powder into a large bowl, stir it, and put it in the refrigerator. As it sits, the cocoa powder will dissolve.

Cool the cake in the pan for at least 10 minutes before inverting it onto a serving plate; peel off the parchment paper. Let it stand until just warm before serving.

To serve, whip the cream and cocoa powder in the chilled bowl until firm peaks form. Serve the chocolate cream alongside slices of cake or let the cake cool completely and frost it with the whipped cocoa cream.

BLOOD ORANGE OLIVE OIL CAKE

½ cup olive oil plus more
for greasing the pan

3 navel blood oranges

¾ cup (divided) plus
2 tablespoons granulated sugar

4 large eggs, separated

½ teaspoon plus a pinch of
fine salt

1 cup self-rising flour

YIELD: 8 SERVINGS

What makes this recipe really sing:
Blood oranges, whose season is in the
dead of winter in the United States,
have a deeper orange and tart flavor and
are a perfect match for grassy olive oil.
Use regular olive oil here; extra-virgin
can be too strong a flavor and
overpower the delicate cake. This moist
cake tastes even better the next day.

What to toss in if you have it:
A scoop of creamy hazelnut gelato
and a sprinkling of toasted hazelnuts
will instantly transport you to a sunny
palazzo in Tuscany.

Preheat the oven to 350°F.

Grease a 9-inch springform cake pan with olive oil.

Zest 1 orange and reserve. With a sharp knife, remove the pith of the
zested orange plus the peel of another one by cutting around the segments
and exposing the flesh. Carefully slice the orange segments away from the
membrane and reserve; squeeze the juice from the membrane into a small
bowl. Scatter the orange segments evenly over the bottom of the cake
pan. In a large bowl, whisk together ½ cup sugar and the egg yolks until
lightened and pale. Add the orange zest, 2 tablespoons orange juice, ½ cup
olive oil, and ½ teaspoon salt and whisk until combined. Fold in the flour
until combined; do not overmix.

In the bowl of an electric mixer, beat the egg whites with a pinch of salt
at medium speed until foamy. Increase the speed to medium high and
gradually sprinkle in 2 tablespoons sugar until soft peaks form. With a
large rubber spatula, fold about a third of the whites into the batter to
lighten; then fold in the remaining whites gently until no white streaks are
visible.

Slowly pour the batter over the oranges and tap the pan gently on a
counter to release any large air bubbles. Bake until golden and a toothpick
inserted into the center of the cake comes out clean, about 40 minutes.

Cool the cake in the pan on a rack for 10 minutes. Remove the outer ring
and let cake cool completely on the pan bottom. Put a large flat plate over
the top of the cake and invert it. Meanwhile, put the remaining ¼ cup
sugar in a small saucepan. Squeeze the juice from the remaining orange
into the pan and bring to a simmer over medium-low heat. Cook until
thick and syrupy, about 10 minutes. Cool completely.

Drizzle the orange syrup evenly over the cake before serving.

STRAWBERRY TART
with BASIL CREAM

1 sheet frozen puff pastry, thawed

1 cup heavy cream

3 tablespoons powdered or confectioners' sugar

¼ cup finely chopped basil leaves plus a few leaves, for garnish

12 large strawberries, hulled and thinly sliced

YIELD: 6 SERVINGS

What makes this recipe really sing:
In the heat of summer, I love the refreshing flavor of fresh herbs and berries. The basil perfumes the slightly sweetened, softly whipped cream and marries so well with the strawberries, and the buttery, flaky puff pastry just puts it all over the top. I call some recipes conversation starters because of their unique combinations. This is one of them.

What to toss in if you have it:
Of course mint is spectacular with strawberries, but I actually love to toss in a bit of mint along with the basil on a really hot day to add a clean, refreshing flavor punch. If you want to make the cream more decadent, fold in some mascarpone cheese. A sprinkle of toasted chopped almonds is nice if you are in a nutty mood. Keep in mind, you are the executive chef of your own kitchen, so play with the berries and herbs in this tart to create a new favorite, tailor-made for your family and friends.

Preheat the oven to 400°F. Line a baking sheet with a silicone baking mat or parchment paper.

On a work surface, roll the puff pastry into a roughly 10 × 16-inch rectangle. With a sharp knife, trim uneven edges to make a perfect rectangle. Evenly cut off the outer 1 inch of each side of the rectangle in strips and set them aside; put the rectangle of puff pastry on the lined baking sheet. Dip your finger in water and run around the outer edges of the rectangle and replace the removed strips of pastry along the edges of the rectangle sheet, forming a wall around the perimeter, pressing lightly to adhere. With a fork, pierce the interior of the tart shell to prevent rising; do not pierce the adhered pastry outer edges. Bake 15 minutes, or until the outer edges have puffed and are golden in color; set aside to cool to room temperature.

In a large bowl, whip the cream until very soft peaks form and begin whisking in the sugar. Gently fold in the chopped basil and chill covered until ready to serve.

To serve, top the cooked puff pastry tart shell with the basil whipped cream. Then place the sliced strawberries overlapping on top of the basil cream. Garnish with a few leaves of fresh basil.

SANTINO'S CRÈME BRÛLÉE

Twenty-four hours before making the brûlée, place whole sprigs of rosemary in the cream and refrigerate.

Preheat the oven to 325°F.

In a heavy-bottomed saucepan over medium-low heat, slowly bring the cream with rosemary, vanilla bean paste, and a pinch of salt to a simmer. Remove from heat and discard rosemary. Set aside.

In a large mixing bowl whisk yolks and 6 tablespoons of sugar. Temper yolks and sugar by slowly pouring in a thin stream of warm cream mixture while whisking. Continue to add the rest of cream mixture to eggs while whisking.

Pour mixture into ramekins placed in a baking dish. Pour warm water in the baking dish until halfway up the outside of the ramekins, making a water bath.

Place in the oven for 30 minutes or until the cream wiggles when shaken. Remove and allow to cool to room temperature. Chill in refrigerator until ready to serve. Just before serving, sprinkle the remaining 2 tablespoons of sugar on top of each baked crème and caramelize with a small kitchen blowtorch or under a broiler on high until golden and caramelized in color.

6 sprigs fresh rosemary

3 cups heavy cream

1/2 teaspoon vanilla bean paste

Pinch of salt

8 egg yolks

8 tablespoons granulated sugar, divided

SPECIAL EQUIPMENT:

6–8 ramekins

YIELD: 6 TO 8 SERVINGS

What makes this recipe really sing:
Are you kidding me? It's rosemary-infused crème brûlée! Definitely a fun conversation starter and a beautiful marriage of flavors. A wonderful home chef that also happens to be an excellent production manager on *Food Network Challenge* made these at the request of his wonderful wife and I was in awe of the unique taste! I had to have the recipe and lo and behold he gave it to me so I can now share it with you. Thank you, Santino!

What to toss in if you have it:
I kind of love this just as it is!

MENU IDEAS *for* MEMORABLE MEALS

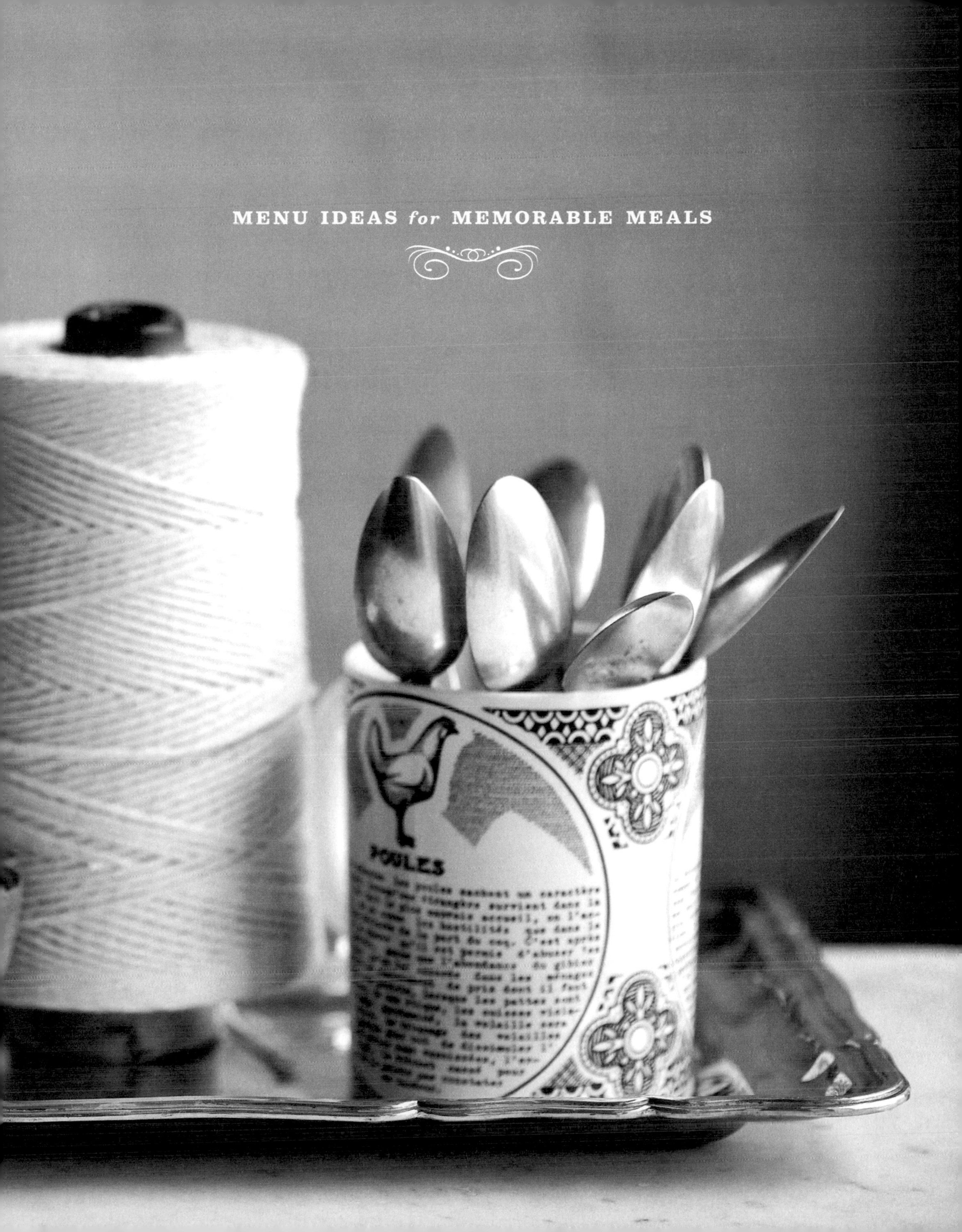

SKIP THE SIT-DOWN COCKTAIL PARTY

‣ Spicy Citrus Mozzarella Bites

‣ Fig and Rosemary Flatbread

‣ Rosemary-Parmesan Shortbread

‣ Atticus' Asparagus Pesto Bites

VEGGIN' OUT

‣ Mushroom Carpaccio

‣ Fig and Blue Cheese Tart

‣ Roasted Beets with Oranges
  and Goat Cheese

‣ Roasted Pineapple with
  Thyme-Ginger Ice

CASUAL FRIDAY NIGHT

‣ Easy White Pizza

‣ Zucchini Ribbon Salad

‣ Millionaire's Shortbread

SOUTHERN DINNER BELL

‣ Spicy Pecan and Parmesan
  Cheese Straws

‣ Classic Southern Blackened Catfish

‣ Tomato and Vidalia Onion Gratin

‣ Grandma Moore's Creamed Corn

‣ Bananas Foster

FALLING FOR A CELEBRATION

‣ Pork Roast with Hard Cider Gravy

‣ Ricotta-Thyme Spaetzle

‣ Smoky Collard Greens

‣ Chai Spiced S'mores

LET US GIVE THANKS

‣ Roasted Turkey Breast with Gravy

‣ Cornbread Dressing

‣ Nutty Green Beans with Blue
  Cheese and Bacon

‣ Spiced Stone Fruit Chutney

‣ Ginger Pumpkin Tart

THE LIGHTER SIDE OF THE HOLIDAYS

‣ Cornish Hens au Vin

‣ Wild Rice Casserole

‣ Gingered Butternut Squash Flambé

‣ Poached Pears with Creamy
  Pecan Sauce

FROSTY EVENING GATHERING

‣ Ginger and Lemon Roasted Chicken
  with Braised Fennel

‣ Maple Whipped Sweet Potatoes
  with Caramelized Onions

‣ Sauteed Wild Mushrooms

‣ Flourless Chocolate-Lover's Cake

PERFECT POTLUCK DISHES

- Indian Corn with Curry Yogurt
- Meat Pies
- Walnut-Sage Potato Gratin
- German Potatoes
- Brown Butter Banana Muffins
- Blood Orange Olive Oil Cake

WHEN SPRING HAS SPRUNG

- Classic Roasted Leg of Lamb
- Easy Ratatouille
- Grilled Romaine Spears with Citrus Vinaigrette
- White Chocolate Mousse

SUMMER GET-TOGETHER

- Dry-Rubbed BBQ Chicken
- BBQ Sauce (jar and give to guests as a takeaway)
- Classic Coleslaw
- Classic Bourbon Baked Beans
- Frozen Lemon Whip with Blueberry Sauce

SHOWIN' OFF DINNER

- Rib Eye Steaks au Poivre
- Rich Porcini Mushroom Risotto
- Asparagus with Balsamic Browned Butter
- Chocolate Pots de Crème with Cherry Whip

FOR THE KID IN EVERYONE

- Buttermilk Pecan Chicken
- Fennel, Strawberry, and Arugula Salad
- Cheesy Penne
- Prosecco Gelatin Parfait
- Pomegranate-Lemon Spritzers (minus the vodka)

BOUNTIFUL BRUNCH

- Maple Candied Bacon
- Spinach and Eggs en Cocotte
- Brown Butter Banana Muffins
- Pumpkin Seed Dried-Cherry Trail Mix

A Letter of Thanks

I RECENTLY CAME ACROSS A RECIPE JOURNAL from my childhood. Each ingredient was written in a different brightly colored pen with lots of doodling in the margins. I realized how long the journey has been to reach this point. I have had the great fortune of so many people's influence, guidance, and help along the way, and I am more than grateful to all of them.

I thank all of my wonderful family for supporting my dreams throughout the years. Mama, I thank you for letting me "experiment" in the kitchen without even the slightest hesitation. You are the foundation to my success, and I love you very much! XOXO Thank you to my friends Sarah Reardon, April Panitz, and Shannon Olivas, for being my cheering section and offering a shoulder when needed, but especially for being as special as each of you are and inspiring me every single day!

Thanks to the incredible team of people at William Morris Endeavor for being the cornerstone of guidance in each venture I pursue. Suzanne Gluck and Andy McNicol, I thank you for all your patience and excitement. Mark Mullett, you have held my hand during each and every step and I am eternally grateful!

I especially want to thank the team of rock stars behind the shows we all love on the Food Network: Bob Tuschman, Allison Page, and Brian Lando. Beth Burke, you are my hero and your energy is contagious! I feel so fortunate to work with you every day. FaYu, you have been such a consistent source of encouragement, and you are so talented in all that you touch. I am incredibly lucky to work with every person at Food Network, and a "thank you" is truly not enough for all that each of you do.

Thank you to Rock Shrimp Productions for giving me a welcome home and having the most amazing spirit! Kim Martin and Fran Alswang, ya'll are just awesome! Thanks to Bobby Flay for being an awe-inspiring chef and exceptional mentor through each step of this experience. A huge thanks to the entire, super-talented team behind the show *5 Ingredient Fix*. You all are my house of fortitude.

Many, many, many thanks to Grand Central Publishing for believing in me and being more than saints as I put together my first book. Karen Murgolo and Matthew Ballast, what can I say? You both have been angels! I thank you for all of your patience, guidance, support, attitude, and borrowed strength. Karen, I appreciate the wonderful light you've shone on this process for me.

And thank you to Sara Ceglarski for helping me find the right words. And many thanks to the most fabulous crew that made this book come to life! Wes Martin, Steven Murello, Abby Jenkins Boal, and Kevin Mendlin. We did it!

Index

About the Author

CLAIRE ROBINSON IS THE HOST OF FOOD Network's *5 Ingredient Fix* and *Food Network Challenge*. She cites her French-speaking grandmother as a major influence on her love for food. Claire graduated from the French Culinary Institute, is an accomplished private chef, and has worked on culinary production teams for several cooking series including Food Network's *Easy Entertaining with Michael Chiarello*. She lives in Brooklyn, New York.